BREAKING THE SILENCE
A JOURNEY THROUGH MENTAL HEALTH

Table of Contents

INTRODUCTION

Mental health is an integral component of our overall well-being, yet it remains one of the most misunderstood and neglected areas of health. As society progresses, the recognition of mental health's importance grows, but significant challenges remain in eradicating the stigma and providing adequate support for those affected. "Breaking the Silence: A Journey Through Mental Health" aims to shed light on the multifaceted nature of mental health, from understanding its basic principles to exploring the global landscape of mental health advocacy.

The journey to understanding mental health begins with defining what it is and why it matters. Mental health encompasses our emotional, psychological, and social well-being. It affects how we think, feel, and act, influencing how we handle stress, relate to others, and make choices. Mental health is crucial at every stage of life, from childhood and adolescence through adulthood. However, unlike physical health, mental health issues often go unnoticed or unacknowledged due to various reasons, including societal stigma and a lack of awareness.

The stigma surrounding mental health is a significant barrier to individuals seeking help. Historically, mental health disorders were often misunderstood and associated with negative stereotypes, leading to discrimination and social exclusion. This stigma not only affects those suffering from mental health issues but also discourages open conversations and education on the topic. One of the primary goals of this book is to break down these barriers, encouraging a more open and informed dialogue about mental health.

Education plays a pivotal role in mental health awareness. By incorporating mental health education into school curriculums and workplace training programs, we can equip individuals with the knowledge to recognise early signs of mental health issues and provide appropriate support. Understanding the symptoms and treatment options for various mental health disorders can empower individuals to seek help and support others in their journey towards mental wellness.

The workplace is another critical arena where mental health awareness is essential. With increasing stress levels and demanding work environments, employees' mental health can significantly impact productivity and overall workplace harmony. Employers have a responsibility to foster a supportive environment that promotes mental well-being, offering resources and support systems for employees struggling with mental health issues.

Youth mental health is a particularly pressing issue, as early intervention can prevent the development of more severe mental health problems later in life. Adolescents and young adults face unique challenges, including academic pressures, social dynamics, and the transition to adulthood. Providing mental health resources and support for young people is crucial for their development and long-term well-being.

As individuals age, mental health remains a vital aspect of their overall health. The elderly population faces specific mental health challenges, such as dealing with loss, physical health decline, and isolation. Addressing the mental health needs of the elderly requires a tailored approach that considers these unique factors and provides appropriate support.

Support systems, both formal and informal, play a crucial role in mental health. Family, friends, and community networks can offer emotional support and practical assistance, while professional services provide specialised care and treatment. The synergy between these support systems can significantly enhance an individual's mental health journey.

Therapeutic approaches to mental health have evolved over the years, offering various treatment options such as psychotherapy, medication, and alternative therapies. Understanding these approaches can help individuals make informed decisions about their treatment plans and find the most suitable path to recovery.

Policy and advocacy are fundamental to driving systemic changes in mental health care. Government policies, funding, and legislation play a critical role in shaping mental health services and accessibility. Advocacy efforts can influence these policies, ensuring that mental health is prioritised and adequately resourced.

Community-based mental health programs offer a grassroots approach to support mental well-being. These programs are often tailored to meet the specific needs of local communities, providing accessible and culturally appropriate services.

The global perspective on mental health highlights the disparities and commonalities across different regions and cultures. By examining mental health practices worldwide, we can learn from successful models and implement strategies that resonate within our own communities.

Looking to the future, the landscape of mental health advocacy is poised for significant transformation. Technological advancements, increased awareness, and evolving societal attitudes promise a more inclusive and supportive environment for those affected by mental health issues.

Finally, personal stories of triumph and resilience serve as powerful reminders of the strength of the human spirit. These narratives offer hope and inspiration, showing that recovery and a fulfilling life are possible despite mental health challenges.

"Breaking the Silence: A Journey Through Mental Health" invites readers to embark on a comprehensive exploration of mental health, encouraging understanding, empathy, and action. By breaking the silence and fostering a more informed and compassionate society, we can create a world where mental health is openly discussed, adequately supported, and universally valued.

CHAPTER 1: UNDERSTANDING MENTAL HEALTH

Mental health is a crucial aspect of overall well-being, encompassing emotional, psychological, and social factors. It influences how we think, feel, and behave, shaping our interactions with others and our approach to life's challenges. Understanding mental health requires a holistic view that considers biological, psychological, and social dimensions.

Defining Mental Health

Mental health is often defined as a state of well-being in which an individual realises their own abilities, can cope with the normal stresses of life, work productively, and contribute to their community. It is more than just the absence of mental disorders; it involves the presence of positive characteristics, such as resilience, self-esteem, and emotional stability.

Biological Factors

Biological factors, including genetics and neurochemistry, play a significant role in mental health. Research has shown that mental health disorders can run in families, indicating a genetic predisposition. Additionally, imbalances in brain chemicals, such as neurotransmitters, are linked to conditions like depression and anxiety.

Psychological Factors

Psychological factors, such as personality traits, coping mechanisms, and past experiences, also impact mental health. For instance, individuals with certain personality traits, like perfectionism or a tendency towards negative thinking, may be more susceptible to mental health issues. Childhood trauma, abuse, or neglect can leave lasting scars, increasing the risk of developing mental disorders later in life.

Social Factors

Social factors, including relationships, culture, and socioeconomic status, significantly influence mental health. Strong, supportive relationships can provide a buffer against stress and promote mental well-being, while social isolation and loneliness can have detrimental effects. Cultural norms and societal expectations can shape how individuals perceive and respond to mental health issues. Socioeconomic factors, such as poverty and unemployment, are also linked to higher rates of mental health problems.

Mental Health Continuum

Mental health exists on a continuum, ranging from optimal well-being to severe mental illness. At one end of the spectrum, individuals experience positive mental health, characterised by high levels of functioning and resilience. At the other end, individuals may suffer from mental health disorders that significantly impair their daily lives.

Optimal Mental Health

Individuals with optimal mental health generally have a positive outlook on life, can manage stress effectively, and maintain fulfilling relationships. They possess a sense of purpose and meaning, and they are capable of adapting to change and overcoming adversity.

Mild to Moderate Mental Health Issues

Many people experience mild to moderate mental health issues at some point in their lives. These issues can include feelings of sadness, anxiety, or stress, which may be temporary and related to specific situations. While these feelings are common, they can still impact daily functioning and quality of life if not addressed.

Severe Mental Health Disorders

Severe mental health disorders, such as major depression, bipolar disorder, schizophrenia, and severe anxiety disorders, can profoundly affect an individual's life. These conditions often require professional intervention and ongoing treatment to manage symptoms and improve quality of life.

Common Mental Health Disorders

Understanding common mental health disorders is essential for recognising symptoms and seeking appropriate help. Some of the most prevalent disorders include:

Depression

Depression is characterised by persistent feelings of sadness, hopelessness, and a lack of interest or pleasure in activities. It can affect sleep, appetite, and energy levels, making it difficult to carry out daily tasks. Depression is more than just feeling sad; it is a serious condition that requires treatment.

Anxiety Disorders

Anxiety disorders encompass a range of conditions, including generalised anxiety disorder (GAD), panic disorder, social anxiety disorder, and specific phobias. These disorders involve excessive fear or worry that can interfere with daily activities. Symptoms may include restlessness, rapid heartbeat, and difficulty concentrating.

Bipolar Disorder

Bipolar disorder is characterised by extreme mood swings, including periods of mania (elevated mood and energy) and depression. These mood shifts can be severe and affect an individual's ability to function. Treatment often involves medication and psychotherapy to stabilise mood fluctuations.

Schizophrenia

Schizophrenia is a chronic mental health disorder that affects how a person thinks, feels, and behaves. Symptoms can include hallucinations, delusions, and disorganised thinking. Schizophrenia requires long-term treatment, often combining medication with therapy and support services.

The Impact of Mental Health

Mental health significantly impacts all areas of life, including physical health, relationships, and productivity. Poor mental health can lead to a decline in physical health, as stress and mental illness can contribute to various conditions such as heart disease, obesity, and weakened immune function. Conversely, good mental health promotes better physical health, as individuals are more likely to engage in healthy behaviours and manage stress effectively.

Physical Health

Mental health and physical health are deeply interconnected. Chronic stress, for example, can lead to physical symptoms such as headaches, high blood pressure, and gastrointestinal issues. Individuals with mental health disorders may also experience sleep disturbances, fatigue, and a lack of energy, which can further impact their physical well-being. Moreover, poor mental health can result in neglect of personal health, including irregular eating habits, lack of exercise, and substance abuse.

Relationships

Mental health significantly affects relationships with family, friends, and colleagues. Individuals struggling with mental health issues may find it challenging to maintain healthy relationships due to mood swings, irritability, or withdrawal. They may also face difficulties in communication, leading to misunderstandings and conflicts. On the other hand, supportive relationships can enhance mental health by providing emotional support, reducing feelings of isolation, and fostering a sense of belonging.

Productivity

Mental health also plays a crucial role in productivity and performance. In the workplace, employees with good mental health are generally more engaged, motivated, and effective in their roles. Conversely, mental health issues such as anxiety, depression, or burnout can impair concentration, decision-making, and overall job performance. This not only affects the individual but can also have broader implications for team dynamics and organisational success.

The Importance of Early Intervention

Recognising and addressing mental health issues early is essential for preventing more severe problems and promoting long-term well-being. Early intervention can involve self-help strategies, such as regular exercise, mindfulness practices, and maintaining a healthy lifestyle. It can also include seeking professional help, such as counselling or therapy, to address underlying issues and develop coping strategies.

Barriers to Mental Health Care

Despite the importance of mental health care, various barriers can prevent individuals from seeking help. These barriers include stigma, lack of awareness, limited access to services, and financial constraints.

Stigma

Stigma remains one of the most significant obstacles to mental health care. Many individuals fear judgement or discrimination if they disclose their mental health issues, leading to reluctance in seeking help. Public education and awareness campaigns are crucial in reducing stigma and promoting a more supportive environment.

Lack of Awareness

Lack of awareness about mental health issues and available resources can also hinder individuals from seeking help. Education on mental health, including recognising symptoms and understanding treatment options, is vital for empowering individuals to take action.

Limited Access to Services

Access to mental health services can be limited by geographic location, availability of professionals, and healthcare infrastructure.

In many rural or underserved areas, mental health services may be scarce, making it challenging for individuals to receive the care they need. Increasing the availability of mental health services, including through telehealth options, can help bridge this gap.

Financial Constraints

Financial constraints can also prevent individuals from accessing mental health care. Therapy sessions, medications, and other treatments can be expensive, and not all insurance plans provide adequate coverage. Advocating for better mental health coverage and affordable care is essential for ensuring that everyone has access to the support they need.

Promoting Mental Health and Well-being

Promoting mental health and well-being requires a multifaceted approach that includes individual actions, community support, and systemic changes. At the individual level, self-care practices such as regular exercise, balanced nutrition, sufficient sleep, and stress management techniques can enhance mental well-being. Building strong relationships and seeking social support are also crucial for maintaining good mental health.

Community Support

Communities play a vital role in supporting mental health. Creating safe, inclusive environments where individuals feel valued and supported can significantly impact mental well-being. Community-based programs, peer support groups, and local mental health initiatives can provide accessible resources and foster a sense of belonging.

Systemic Changes

Systemic changes are necessary to address the broader determinants of mental health. This includes advocating for policies that promote mental health equity, improving access to mental health services, and ensuring that mental health is integrated into all aspects of healthcare. Governments, organisations, and policymakers must work together to create an environment where mental health is prioritised and adequately supported.

Conclusion

Understanding mental health is the first step towards fostering a more inclusive and supportive society. By recognising the various factors that influence mental health and addressing the barriers to care, we can promote better mental well-being for all individuals. Mental health is not just a personal issue; it is a collective responsibility that requires awareness, empathy, and action from everyone in the community.

In the following chapters, we will delve deeper into the history of mental health advocacy, the stigma surrounding mental health, and the various approaches to promoting mental well-being. Through this journey, we aim to break the silence and create a more informed and compassionate society.

CHAPTER 2: THE HISTORY OF MENTAL HEALTH ADVOCACY

Introduction

The history of mental health advocacy is a complex and evolving narrative that reflects the changing perceptions, treatments, and policies surrounding mental health. From ancient times to the modern era, society's approach to mental health has undergone significant transformations. This chapter explores the journey of mental health advocacy, highlighting key milestones, influential figures, and pivotal moments that have shaped the current landscape of mental health awareness and support.

Ancient and Medieval Periods

In ancient civilisations, mental health issues were often misunderstood and attributed to supernatural forces or divine punishment. Ancient Egyptians, Greeks, and Romans had varied approaches to mental health, ranging from philosophical musings to rudimentary medical treatments.

Ancient Civilisations

In ancient Egypt, mental health conditions were often seen as manifestations of spiritual imbalance. Treatments included rituals, prayers, and sometimes physical interventions like trepanation (the drilling of holes into the skull) to release evil spirits. Similarly, in ancient Greece, Hippocrates, the father of modern medicine, proposed that mental health issues were due to imbalances in bodily fluids or "humours." He advocated for treatments like diet, exercise, and bloodletting to restore balance.

Medieval Period

During the medieval period, mental health conditions were frequently associated with witchcraft, demonic possession, and sin. This era saw the rise of asylums, which were often more akin to prisons than places of healing. People with mental health issues were subjected to harsh treatments and confinement, reflecting societal fear and misunderstanding.

The Renaissance and Enlightenment

The Renaissance and Enlightenment periods marked a shift towards more humane and scientific approaches to mental health. These eras laid the groundwork for modern mental health advocacy.

Renaissance

In the Renaissance, there was a renewed interest in the human mind and body. Scholars and physicians began to challenge the prevailing supernatural explanations for mental health issues. Notable figures like Paracelsus and Johann Weyer argued for more compassionate treatments and recognised that mental health conditions were medical issues rather than moral failings.

Enlightenment

The Enlightenment further advanced the understanding of mental health. Philosophers and scientists emphasised reason, observation, and empirical evidence. Philippe Pinel, a French physician, is often credited with pioneering moral treatment in the late 18th century. He advocated for the humane treatment of patients, unchaining them from asylums, and promoting activities that fostered recovery and dignity.

19th Century Reforms

The 19th century saw significant reforms in mental health care, driven by advocates who recognised the need for compassionate and effective treatment.

Asylum Reform Movement

The asylum reform movement, led by figures such as Dorothea Dix in the United States and John Conolly in the United Kingdom, sought to improve the conditions of mental health facilities. Dix's tireless advocacy led to the establishment of more than 30 mental hospitals in the US. Conolly implemented non-restraint policies at the Hanwell Asylum, demonstrating that patients could be managed without physical restraints.

Emergence of Psychiatry

The 19th century also witnessed the formalisation of psychiatry as a medical specialty. Emil Kraepelin, a German psychiatrist, made significant contributions by classifying mental disorders and recognising their biological underpinnings. His work laid the foundation for modern diagnostic criteria and treatment approaches.

Early 20th Century: Psychoanalysis and Institutionalisation

The early 20th century was marked by the rise of psychoanalysis and the continued expansion of institutional care.

Sigmund Freud and Psychoanalysis

Sigmund Freud, an Austrian neurologist, revolutionised the understanding of mental health with his development of psychoanalysis. Freud's theories on the unconscious mind, childhood experiences, and therapeutic techniques like talk therapy influenced the treatment of mental health issues. Psychoanalysis emphasised the importance of exploring unconscious conflicts and past experiences to alleviate mental distress.

Institutionalisation

Despite advances in understanding mental health, the early 20th century saw the proliferation of large psychiatric institutions. These institutions often struggled with overcrowding, inadequate funding, and poor living conditions. Patients were frequently subjected to invasive and experimental treatments, such as electroconvulsive therapy (ECT) and lobotomy, which were sometimes administered without proper consent or regard for patient well-being.

Mid to Late 20th Century: Deinstitutionalisation and Community Care

The mid to late 20th century witnessed a paradigm shift towards deinstitutionalisation and the development of community-based mental health care.

Deinstitutionalisation

The deinstitutionalisation movement, which began in the 1950s and 1960s, aimed to reduce reliance on large psychiatric hospitals and integrate individuals with mental health conditions into the community. This movement was driven by various factors, including the availability of antipsychotic medications, growing awareness of patients' rights, and recognition of the inadequacies of institutional care. Prominent figures like Dr. John F. Kennedy, who signed the Community Mental Health Act in 1963, played a crucial role in advocating for community-based mental health services.

Development of Community Mental Health Services

The shift towards community care emphasised the importance of providing mental health services in more accessible and supportive environments. Community mental health centres were established to offer a range of services, including outpatient treatment, crisis intervention, and rehabilitation programs. This approach aimed to promote independence, reduce stigma, and enhance the quality of life for individuals with mental health conditions.

Modern Era: Advocacy and Rights

The modern era of mental health advocacy is characterised by increased recognition of mental health as a fundamental human right, greater awareness, and ongoing efforts to address stigma and improve access to care.

Rise of Mental Health Advocacy Organisations

Numerous advocacy organisations have emerged to champion mental health causes. Groups such as the National Alliance on Mental Illness (NAMI), Mental Health America, and Mind in the UK have been instrumental in raising awareness, providing support, and advocating for policy changes. These organisations work to empower individuals, promote education, and influence legislation to improve mental health care.

Global Initiatives

Mental health advocacy has also gained traction on the global stage. The World Health Organisation (WHO) has prioritised mental health as a critical component of overall health, launching initiatives to integrate mental health into primary care and promote mental health awareness worldwide. Campaigns like World Mental Health Day, observed on October 10th, aim to educate the public and reduce stigma.

Technological Advancements

The advent of technology has revolutionised mental health advocacy and care. Telehealth services, online support groups, and mental health apps have made it easier for individuals to access information and support. Social media platforms have also provided a space for people to share their experiences, connect with others, and advocate for change.

Conclusion

The history of mental health advocacy is a testament to the enduring efforts of individuals and organisations committed to improving the lives of those affected by mental health conditions. From ancient misconceptions to modern advancements, the journey has been marked by significant progress and ongoing challenges. By understanding this history, we can appreciate the strides that have been made and recognise the work that still needs to be done. As we move forward, continued advocacy, education, and systemic change are essential to ensure that mental health is universally recognised, supported, and prioritised.

CHAPTER 3: RECOGNISING MENTAL HEALTH DISORDERS

Introduction

Recognising mental health disorders is a critical step towards providing appropriate support and treatment. Mental health disorders encompass a wide range of conditions that affect an individual's thinking, mood, and behaviour. Understanding the symptoms and characteristics of these disorders can help individuals seek help early, reduce the impact on their lives, and promote better mental health outcomes. This chapter will explore the various types of mental health disorders, their symptoms, and the importance of early recognition and intervention.

Common Mental Health Disorders

Mental health disorders can vary significantly in terms of their symptoms, severity, and impact on daily life. Some of the most common mental health disorders include depression, anxiety disorders, bipolar disorder, schizophrenia, and eating disorders.

Depression

Depression is one of the most prevalent mental health disorders, characterised by persistent feelings of sadness, hopelessness, and a lack of interest or pleasure in activities. Symptoms of depression can include:

- Persistent sad, anxious, or "empty" mood

- Loss of interest or pleasure in hobbies and activities

- Fatigue or decreased energy

- Difficulty concentrating, remembering, or making decisions

- Insomnia or oversleeping

- Appetite changes, leading to weight loss or gain

- Thoughts of death or suicide

Recognising these symptoms is crucial, as early intervention can prevent the condition from worsening and help individuals regain their quality of life.

Anxiety Disorders

Anxiety disorders are characterised by excessive fear or worry that can interfere with daily activities. These disorders include generalised anxiety disorder (GAD), panic disorder, social anxiety disorder, and specific phobias. Common symptoms of anxiety disorders include:

- Persistent worry or fear

- Restlessness or feeling on edge

- Rapid heartbeat or palpitations

- Sweating, trembling, or shaking

- Shortness of breath

- Avoidance of situations that trigger anxiety

- Difficulty concentrating or sleeping

Identifying anxiety disorders early can help individuals develop coping strategies and reduce the impact of anxiety on their daily lives.

Bipolar Disorder

Bipolar disorder involves extreme mood swings, including episodes of mania (elevated mood and energy) and depression. Symptoms of mania can include:

- Increased energy or activity levels

- Euphoric or irritable mood

- Decreased need for sleep

- Racing thoughts or rapid speech

- Impulsivity or risky behaviour

Symptoms of depressive episodes in bipolar disorder mirror those of major depression. Early recognition and treatment can help individuals manage their symptoms and maintain stability.

Schizophrenia

Schizophrenia is a severe mental health disorder that affects how a person thinks, feels, and behaves. Symptoms of schizophrenia can include:

- Hallucinations (hearing or seeing things that are not there)

- Delusions (false beliefs that are not based in reality)

- Disorganised thinking or speech

- Social withdrawal

- Lack of motivation or emotional expression

- Difficulty functioning in daily life

Early intervention in schizophrenia is critical, as it can improve long-term outcomes and reduce the severity of symptoms.

Eating Disorders

Eating disorders, such as anorexia nervosa, bulimia nervosa, and binge-eating disorder, involve preoccupation with food, body weight, and shape. Symptoms of eating disorders can include:

- Extreme restriction of food intake (anorexia nervosa)

- Binge eating followed by purging (bulimia nervosa)

- Eating large amounts of food in a short period (binge-eating disorder)

- Distorted body image

- Intense fear of gaining weight

Recognising eating disorders early can help prevent serious health complications and support recovery.

Recognising Less Common Mental Health Disorders

In addition to common mental health disorders, there are several less common but equally important conditions that require attention and understanding.

Obsessive-Compulsive Disorder (OCD)

Obsessive-Compulsive Disorder (OCD) is characterised by recurring, unwanted thoughts (obsessions) and repetitive behaviours (compulsions). Symptoms of OCD can include:

- Repeated, intrusive thoughts or images

- Compulsive behaviours performed to alleviate anxiety, such as hand washing, checking, or counting

- Recognition that obsessions and compulsions are excessive or irrational

- Significant distress or impairment in daily functioning

Early recognition and treatment of OCD can help individuals manage their symptoms and reduce the impact on their lives.

Post-Traumatic Stress Disorder (PTSD)

Post-Traumatic Stress Disorder (PTSD) can develop after experiencing or witnessing a traumatic event. Symptoms of PTSD can include:

- Flashbacks or nightmares about the traumatic event

- Avoidance of reminders of the trauma

- Hypervigilance or heightened startle response

- Emotional numbness or detachment

- Difficulty sleeping or concentrating

Early intervention in PTSD can help individuals process their trauma and reduce long-term psychological effects.

Borderline Personality Disorder (BPD)

Borderline Personality Disorder (BPD) is characterised by unstable moods, behaviour, and relationships. Symptoms of BPD can include:

- Intense and unstable relationships

- Impulsive or self-destructive behaviour

- Fear of abandonment

- Severe mood swings

- Chronic feelings of emptiness

- Difficulty managing anger

Recognising BPD early can help individuals access appropriate therapy and support to improve their quality of life.

The Importance of Early Recognition and Intervention

Early recognition and intervention are crucial in managing mental health disorders. Identifying symptoms early can lead to timely treatment, which can prevent the worsening of symptoms and improve overall outcomes. There are several key steps to recognising and addressing mental health disorders:

Awareness and Education

Increasing awareness and education about mental health can help individuals recognise symptoms in themselves and others. Public health campaigns, school programs, and workplace training can all contribute to a greater understanding of mental health disorders and reduce stigma.

Regular Check-Ins

Regular check-ins with oneself and loved ones can help identify changes in mood, behaviour, or functioning that may indicate a mental health issue. Encouraging open conversations about mental health can create a supportive environment where individuals feel comfortable seeking help.

Seeking Professional Help

If symptoms of a mental health disorder are identified, seeking professional help is essential. Mental health professionals, such as psychiatrists, psychologists, and counsellors, can provide accurate diagnoses and develop appropriate treatment plans. Treatment may include therapy, medication, lifestyle changes, or a combination of these approaches.

Support Systems

Building and maintaining strong support systems can significantly impact mental health. Support from family, friends, and community networks can provide emotional and practical assistance, reduce feelings of isolation, and encourage adherence to treatment plans.

Overcoming Barriers to Recognition

Despite the importance of recognising mental health disorders, several barriers can impede this process. These barriers include stigma, lack of awareness, and difficulty accessing mental health services.

Stigma

Stigma surrounding mental health can prevent individuals from acknowledging their symptoms and seeking help. Efforts to reduce stigma, such as public education campaigns and promoting positive portrayals of mental health in the media, are crucial for encouraging early recognition and intervention.

Lack of Awareness

Lack of awareness about mental health disorders and their symptoms can hinder recognition. Providing education about the signs and symptoms of mental health conditions can empower individuals to seek help when needed.

Access to Services

Limited access to mental health services can prevent individuals from receiving timely diagnoses and treatment. Increasing the availability of mental health services, particularly in underserved areas, and integrating mental health care into primary health care systems can help address this barrier.

Conclusion

Recognising mental health disorders is a vital step in promoting mental health and well-being. Understanding the symptoms and characteristics of various mental health conditions can help individuals seek help early, reducing the impact on their lives and improving outcomes. By increasing awareness, reducing stigma, and enhancing access to mental health services, we can create a more supportive and responsive environment for those affected by mental health disorders.

CHAPTER 4: THE STIGMA SURROUNDING MENTAL HEALTH

Introduction

Stigma surrounding mental health remains one of the most significant barriers to addressing mental health issues effectively. Stigma can manifest in various ways, including negative stereotypes, discrimination, and social exclusion, which can prevent individuals from seeking help and receiving the support they need. This chapter explores the origins of mental health stigma, its impact on individuals and society, and the steps we can take to combat it.

The Origins of Mental Health Stigma

Stigma surrounding mental health has deep historical roots, often stemming from misconceptions, fear, and lack of understanding. Throughout history, mental health conditions have been misunderstood and misrepresented, leading to the development of negative attitudes and beliefs.

Historical Misconceptions

In ancient and medieval times, mental health issues were frequently attributed to supernatural causes, such as demonic possession or divine punishment. These beliefs led to harsh and inhumane treatments, including exorcisms, isolation, and physical restraints. As a result, individuals with mental health conditions were often feared, marginalised, and treated as outcasts.

The Role of Media and Popular Culture

Media and popular culture have played a significant role in perpetuating mental health stigma. Misrepresentations of mental health conditions in films, television shows, and news stories have often portrayed individuals with mental health issues as dangerous, unpredictable, or incompetent. These portrayals contribute to public fear and misunderstanding, reinforcing negative stereotypes.

Types of Stigmas

Stigma can be broadly categorised into public stigma, self-stigma, and structural stigma, each of which affects individuals and society in different ways.

Public Stigma

Public stigma refers to the negative attitudes and beliefs held by the general public towards individuals with mental health conditions. This type of stigma can lead to discrimination, social exclusion, and a lack of empathy and support. Public stigma is often reinforced by stereotypes and misinformation, creating a hostile environment for those affected by mental health issues.

Self-Stigma

Self-stigma occurs when individuals internalise public stigma and begin to believe the negative stereotypes about themselves. This can lead to feelings of shame, guilt, and low self-esteem, which can further exacerbate mental health conditions. Self-stigma can also prevent individuals from seeking help, as they may fear judgement or believe that they are unworthy of support.

Structural Stigma

Structural stigma refers to systemic policies, practices, and cultural norms that discriminate against individuals with mental health conditions. This can include inadequate mental health funding, limited access to services, and discriminatory policies in workplaces, schools, and healthcare settings. Structural stigma perpetuates inequality and limits opportunities for individuals with mental health issues.

The Impact of Stigma on Mental Health

Stigma has profound and far-reaching effects on individuals with mental health conditions, as well as on society as a whole. These impacts can be seen in various areas, including help-seeking behaviour, treatment outcomes, and overall quality of life.

Help-Seeking Behaviour

One of the most significant effects of stigma is its impact on help-seeking behaviour. Fear of judgement, discrimination, and social exclusion can prevent individuals from seeking the help they need. This reluctance to seek support can delay diagnosis and treatment, leading to worsening symptoms and a decline in mental health.

Treatment Outcomes

Stigma can also affect treatment outcomes by influencing the quality of care that individuals receive. Healthcare professionals may hold stigmatizing attitudes, which can result in inadequate or biased treatment. Additionally, individuals who internalise stigma may be less likely to adhere to treatment plans, reducing the effectiveness of interventions.

Quality of Life

The negative effects of stigma extend beyond mental health to impact overall quality of life. Individuals who experience stigma may face social isolation, difficulties in maintaining employment, and challenges in building and sustaining relationships. This can lead to a cycle of disadvantage, where the effects of stigma further exacerbate mental health conditions and reduce opportunities for recovery.

Combating Mental Health Stigma

Addressing and reducing mental health stigma requires a multifaceted approach that involves individuals, communities, and broader societal change. Key strategies include education and awareness, promoting positive portrayals of mental health, and advocating for policy changes.

Education and Awareness

Increasing education and awareness about mental health is crucial for reducing stigma. Public health campaigns, school programs, and community initiatives can provide accurate information about mental health conditions, challenge myths and misconceptions, and promote understanding and empathy. By normalising conversations about mental health, we can create a more supportive and inclusive environment.

Promoting Positive Portrayals

Promoting positive portrayals of mental health in the media and popular culture can help to challenge stereotypes and reduce stigma. Encouraging accurate and respectful representations of mental health conditions in films, television shows, and news stories can influence public attitudes and promote a more balanced understanding. Highlighting stories of recovery and resilience can also inspire hope and demonstrate that individuals with mental health conditions can lead fulfilling lives.

Advocacy and Policy Change

Advocacy and policy change are essential for addressing structural stigma and ensuring that individuals with mental health conditions have equal access to opportunities and support. This includes advocating for increased funding for mental health services, implementing anti-discrimination policies in workplaces and schools, and ensuring that mental health is integrated into broader healthcare systems. Policymakers, organisations, and community leaders must work together to create a more equitable and supportive environment for all.

The Role of Individuals and Communities

While systemic change is crucial, individuals and communities also play a vital role in combating mental health stigma. By fostering supportive environments and challenging stigma at a grassroots level, we can make a significant impact.

Building Supportive Environments

Creating supportive environments involves encouraging open conversations about mental health, offering empathy and understanding, and providing practical support to those in need. This can include checking in on friends and family, offering to accompany someone to a medical appointment, or simply being a non-judgemental listener. By showing that mental health is a priority, we can help to reduce the isolation and fear associated with stigma.

Challenging Stigma

Challenging stigma involves speaking out against discriminatory attitudes and behaviours, both in personal interactions and in broader public discourse. This can include correcting misinformation, advocating for inclusive language, and standing up against discrimination in all its forms. By actively challenging stigma, we can contribute to a culture of acceptance and respect.

Conclusion

The stigma surrounding mental health is a pervasive and damaging barrier that affects individuals and society as a whole. Understanding the origins and impacts of stigma is the first step towards addressing this issue. By increasing education and awareness, promoting positive portrayals, advocating for policy change, and fostering supportive environments, we can work together to combat stigma and create a more inclusive and compassionate society. Reducing stigma is not only essential for improving mental health outcomes but also for ensuring that everyone has the opportunity to lead a fulfilling and dignified life.

CHAPTER 5: THE ROLE OF EDUCATION IN MENTAL HEALTH AWARENESS

Introduction

Education plays a pivotal role in promoting mental health awareness and reducing stigma. By integrating mental health education into curricula, public health initiatives, and community programs, we can equip individuals with the knowledge and skills necessary to understand, manage, and support mental health. This chapter explores the significance of mental health education, the various approaches to incorporating it into different settings, and the long-term benefits of an informed and empathetic society.

The Importance of Mental Health Education

Mental health education is essential for several reasons. It helps individuals recognise the signs and symptoms of mental health conditions, understand the importance of seeking help, and learn how to support others. Additionally, education can challenge misconceptions and reduce the stigma associated with mental health issues.

Recognising Signs and Symptoms

Educating individuals about the signs and symptoms of mental health conditions is crucial for early identification and intervention. Awareness of these signs can help people recognise when they or someone else might need support. Common signs and symptoms include changes in mood, behaviour, energy levels, and thinking patterns. Understanding these indicators can prompt timely help-seeking and prevent conditions from worsening.

Encouraging Help-Seeking Behaviour

Mental health education emphasises the importance of seeking help when needed. By normalising conversations about mental health and providing information about available resources, education can reduce the barriers to accessing support. Encouraging help-seeking behaviour is vital for improving mental health outcomes and ensuring individuals receive the care they need.

Supporting Others

Mental health education also teaches individuals how to support others effectively. This includes learning active listening skills, understanding how to offer practical support, and knowing when to encourage professional help. Educating people on how to be empathetic and non-judgemental can create a more supportive environment for those experiencing mental health challenges.

Integrating Mental Health Education into Different Settings

Mental health education can be integrated into various settings, including schools, workplaces, and communities. Each setting offers unique opportunities to reach different populations and promote mental health awareness.

Schools

Schools play a critical role in shaping young people's understanding of mental health. Integrating mental health education into school curricula can have a lasting impact on students' well-being.

Curriculum Integration

Incorporating mental health topics into the curriculum can help students learn about mental health from a young age. This can include lessons on emotional regulation, stress management, and the importance of self-care. Teaching students about mental health alongside traditional subjects can normalise the topic and promote a holistic approach to education.

Teacher Training

Providing teachers with training on mental health can enhance their ability to support students. Training can include recognising signs of mental health issues, knowing how to approach students in distress, and understanding referral pathways for additional support. Educated teachers can create a supportive classroom environment and serve as trusted resources for students.

Peer Support Programs

Implementing peer support programs can empower students to support each other. Peer support programs train students to provide emotional support, share resources, and encourage help-seeking behaviour. These programs can create a sense of community and reduce the stigma associated with mental health issues.

Workplaces

Workplaces are another important setting for mental health education. Promoting mental health awareness in the workplace can improve employee well-being, productivity, and overall organisational health.

Mental Health Training for Managers

Training managers on mental health can help them support their teams effectively. Managers should be educated on recognising signs of stress and burnout, having conversations about mental health, and providing resources for employees in need. A supportive management approach can create a positive work environment and reduce the stigma associated with mental health issues.

Employee Wellness Programs

Implementing employee wellness programs that include mental health education can promote overall well-being. These programs can offer workshops on stress management, mindfulness, and work-life balance. Providing access to mental health resources, such as counselling services, can also encourage employees to seek support when needed.

Creating a Supportive Culture

Fostering a supportive workplace culture involves promoting open conversations about mental health and reducing stigma. Encouraging employees to share their experiences and providing a safe space for discussions can help normalise mental health issues. Organisations can also implement policies that support mental health, such as flexible working arrangements and mental health days.

Communities

Community-based mental health education can reach a wide audience and promote mental health awareness at a grassroots level. Community programs can be tailored to the needs of specific populations and address local mental health challenges.

Public Health Campaigns

Public health campaigns can raise awareness about mental health and reduce stigma. These campaigns can use various media channels, such as social media, television, and print, to disseminate information about mental health conditions, resources, and support services. Campaigns can also highlight personal stories to humanise mental health issues and promote empathy.

Community Workshops

Hosting community workshops on mental health can provide valuable information and support to local residents. Workshops can cover topics such as stress management, coping strategies, and mental health first aid. Engaging local mental health professionals to lead these workshops can ensure that the information provided is accurate and relevant.

Support Groups

Creating support groups within communities can offer individuals a space to share their experiences and receive support. Support groups can be facilitated by trained professionals or peer leaders and can focus on specific mental health issues or general well-being. These groups can foster a sense of belonging and reduce feelings of isolation.

The Long-Term Benefits of Mental Health Education

Investing in mental health education can have long-term benefits for individuals and society. These benefits include improved mental health outcomes, reduced stigma, and enhanced overall well-being.

Improved Mental Health Outcomes

By increasing awareness and understanding of mental health, education can lead to earlier identification and intervention. Early support can prevent mental health conditions from worsening and improve recovery rates. Educated individuals are also more likely to seek help and adhere to treatment plans, leading to better long-term outcomes.

Reduced Stigma

Mental health education can challenge misconceptions and reduce the stigma associated with mental health issues. As more people become informed about mental health, negative attitudes and stereotypes can diminish. Reduced stigma can create a more supportive environment for individuals with mental health conditions and encourage open conversations about mental health.

Enhanced Overall Well-Being

Education on mental health can promote overall well-being by teaching individuals how to manage stress, build resilience, and maintain healthy relationships. These skills are valuable not only for those with mental health conditions but for everyone. A society that prioritises mental health education is likely to experience higher levels of well-being and social cohesion.

Conclusion

The role of education in mental health awareness is multifaceted and crucial for promoting a supportive and informed society. By integrating mental health education into schools, workplaces, and communities, we can equip individuals with the knowledge and skills needed to understand and support mental health. The long-term benefits of mental health education, including improved outcomes, reduced stigma, and enhanced well-being, highlight the importance of continued investment in this area. Through education, we can create a more empathetic and resilient society, better equipped to address the mental health challenges of today and the future.

CHAPTER 6: MENTAL HEALTH IN THE WORKPLACE

Introduction

Mental health in the workplace is an increasingly important issue, affecting not only the well-being of employees but also the overall productivity and success of organisations. A supportive work environment that prioritises mental health can lead to a more engaged, motivated, and resilient workforce. This chapter explores the significance of mental health in the workplace, the factors contributing to workplace stress, and strategies for promoting a mentally healthy work environment.

The Importance of Mental Health in the Workplace

Mental health is a critical component of overall health, and it significantly influences an individual's ability to perform well at work. Poor mental health can lead to decreased productivity, higher absenteeism, and increased turnover rates. Conversely, a workplace that supports mental health can enhance employee satisfaction, improve performance, and foster a positive organisational culture.

Impact on Productivity

Mental health issues such as stress, anxiety, and depression can severely impact an employee's ability to concentrate, make decisions, and complete tasks efficiently. This can lead to reduced productivity and lower quality of work. Employers who invest in mental health support can help mitigate these effects, resulting in a more productive workforce.

Employee Retention

Workplaces that prioritise mental health tend to have higher employee retention rates. When employees feel supported and valued, they are more likely to stay with the organisation. This reduces the costs associated with recruitment and training and helps maintain organisational stability.

Organisational Culture

A focus on mental health contributes to a positive organisational culture where employees feel safe and respected. This can enhance teamwork, communication, and overall morale. A supportive culture also attracts talent, as prospective employees are more likely to choose workplaces that demonstrate a commitment to employee well-being.

Factors Contributing to Workplace Stress

Various factors can contribute to workplace stress and negatively impact mental health. Understanding these factors is essential for developing effective strategies to address them.

Workload and Job Demands

High workloads, tight deadlines, and unrealistic job demands can lead to chronic stress. Employees who feel overwhelmed by their responsibilities may struggle to maintain a work-life balance, leading to burnout and mental health issues.

Lack of Control and Autonomy

Employees who have little control over their work and lack autonomy in decision-making often experience higher levels of stress. Empowering employees to have a say in how they complete their tasks can enhance job satisfaction and reduce stress.

Poor Work Relationships

Negative relationships with colleagues or supervisors can create a toxic work environment. Bullying, harassment, and lack of support can contribute to anxiety, depression, and other mental health problems. Fostering positive relationships and promoting respect in the workplace is crucial for mental well-being.

Job Insecurity

Uncertainty about job stability can cause significant stress. Employees who fear losing their jobs or face unclear career prospects may experience anxiety and decreased motivation. Transparent communication and support during organisational changes can help alleviate these concerns.

Work-Life Imbalance

An imbalance between work and personal life can lead to stress and burnout. Long working hours, lack of flexibility, and insufficient time for rest and personal activities can negatively impact mental health. Promoting a healthy work-life balance is essential for maintaining employee well-being.

Strategies for Promoting Mental Health in the Workplace

Creating a mentally healthy workplace requires a proactive approach that includes policies, programs, and practices designed to support employees' mental health.

Mental Health Policies

Developing and implementing mental health policies is a foundational step in promoting workplace well-being. These policies should outline the organisation's commitment to mental health, define procedures for supporting employees, and provide guidelines for addressing mental health issues.

Clear Communication

Policies should be communicated clearly to all employees, ensuring they understand the support available to them. This includes information on mental health resources, confidentiality, and procedures for requesting accommodations.

Inclusivity and Diversity

Mental health policies should consider the diverse needs of employees. This includes recognising cultural differences in mental health perceptions and ensuring that policies are inclusive and respectful of all backgrounds.

Employee Assistance Programs (EAPs)

Employee Assistance Programs (EAPs) offer confidential counselling and support services for employees facing personal or work-related issues. EAPs can provide valuable resources for managing stress, anxiety, and other mental health challenges.

Access to Professional Support

EAPs connect employees with mental health professionals who can offer counselling, therapy, and other forms of support. Providing easy access to these services encourages employees to seek help when needed.

Promoting EAPs

Organisations should actively promote EAPs and ensure that employees are aware of the services available. Regular communication, such as newsletters and information sessions, can help increase utilisation rates.

Training and Awareness Programs

Training and awareness programs can equip employees and managers with the knowledge and skills to support mental health in the workplace.

Mental Health First Aid

Training employees in mental health first aid can enable them to recognise signs of mental health issues and provide initial support.

This can help create a network of informed individuals who can offer assistance and refer colleagues to professional help.

Manager Training

Training managers to support mental health is crucial for fostering a supportive work environment. Managers should learn how to recognise stress, approach sensitive conversations, and provide accommodations. Effective manager training can lead to better communication and stronger team dynamics.

Promoting Work-Life Balance

Encouraging a healthy work-life balance is essential for preventing burnout and promoting mental well-being.

Flexible Working Arrangements

Offering flexible working arrangements, such as remote work, flexible hours, and part-time options, can help employees balance their personal and professional lives. Flexibility can reduce stress and improve job satisfaction.

Encouraging Time Off

Promoting the use of annual leave and ensuring that employees take breaks can prevent burnout. Organisations should encourage employees to disconnect from work during their time off and avoid a culture of overworking.

Creating a Supportive Environment

Fostering a supportive environment involves creating a culture of empathy, respect, and openness.

Open Communication

Encouraging open communication about mental health can reduce stigma and create a supportive atmosphere. Regular check-ins, team meetings, and anonymous feedback channels can help employees feel heard and valued.

Peer Support Networks

Establishing peer support networks can provide employees with additional resources for mental health support. Peer support groups, mentoring programs, and buddy systems can offer a sense of community and belonging.

The Role of Leadership

Leadership plays a crucial role in promoting mental health in the workplace. Leaders who prioritise mental well-being can set the tone for the entire organisation.

Leading by Example

Leaders should model healthy behaviours by prioritising their own mental health and work-life balance. Demonstrating empathy, taking regular breaks, and being open about mental health can encourage employees to do the same.

Advocacy and Commitment

Leaders should advocate for mental health initiatives and demonstrate a commitment to supporting employee well-being. This includes allocating resources, supporting policy development, and championing mental health programs.

Conclusion

Mental health in the workplace is a vital aspect of overall organisational health and employee well-being. By understanding the factors that contribute to workplace stress and implementing strategies to support mental health, organisations can create a positive and productive work environment. Promoting mental health requires a multifaceted approach, including policies, programs, training, and a supportive culture. With strong leadership and a commitment to mental well-being, workplaces can foster a resilient and engaged workforce, ultimately leading to greater success and satisfaction for both employees and employers.

CHAPTER 7: YOUTH AND MENTAL HEALTH

Introduction

Mental health issues among young people are a growing concern worldwide. Adolescence and young adulthood are critical periods for mental health, as they involve significant physical, emotional, and social changes. This chapter examines the unique mental health challenges faced by young people, the factors contributing to these challenges, and strategies for supporting youth mental health.

The Prevalence of Mental Health Issues in Youth

Mental health issues are common among young people, with many experiencing conditions such as anxiety, depression, and behavioural disorders. According to the World Health Organization, approximately 10-20% of children and adolescents experience mental health conditions, but the majority go undiagnosed and untreated. Early intervention and support are crucial for preventing long-term consequences and promoting positive mental health outcomes.

Factors Contributing to Youth Mental Health Issues

Several factors contribute to the mental health challenges faced by young people. These include biological, psychological, social, and environmental influences.

Biological Factors

Biological factors, such as genetics and brain chemistry, can play a significant role in the development of mental health conditions.

Family history of mental illness can increase the risk of similar issues in young people. Additionally, hormonal changes during puberty can affect mood and behaviour, making adolescents more vulnerable to mental health problems.

Psychological Factors

Psychological factors, including personality traits and coping mechanisms, influence how young people respond to stress and adversity. Low self-esteem, perfectionism, and poor coping skills can contribute to the development of anxiety, depression, and other mental health issues. Developing resilience and healthy coping strategies is essential for managing psychological stressors.

Social Factors

Social factors, such as family dynamics, peer relationships, and school environment, significantly impact youth mental health. Positive relationships with family and friends can provide essential support, while conflict, bullying, and social isolation can lead to mental health problems. The pressure to perform academically and socially can also contribute to stress and anxiety.

Environmental Factors

Environmental factors, including socioeconomic status, access to healthcare, and exposure to trauma, influence mental health. Young people from disadvantaged backgrounds may face additional stressors, such as financial instability and limited access to mental health services. Exposure to violence, abuse, or neglect can have long-lasting effects on mental health.

Common Mental Health Issues Among Youth

Young people can experience a range of mental health issues, each with its own set of symptoms and challenges. Understanding these conditions is essential for providing appropriate support and intervention.

Anxiety Disorders

Anxiety disorders are among the most common mental health conditions in young people. These disorders can manifest as excessive worry, fear, or nervousness that interferes with daily activities. Common types of anxiety disorders include generalised anxiety disorder (GAD), social anxiety disorder, and panic disorder. Symptoms may include restlessness, irritability, difficulty concentrating, and physical symptoms such as headaches or stomach-aches.

Depression

Depression is characterised by persistent feelings of sadness, hopelessness, and a lack of interest or pleasure in activities. Young people with depression may experience changes in appetite and sleep patterns, fatigue, difficulty concentrating, and thoughts of self-harm or suicide. Early intervention and treatment are crucial for preventing the long-term effects of depression.

Behavioural Disorders

Behavioural disorders, such as attention-deficit/hyperactivity disorder (ADHD) and conduct disorder, can impact young people's ability to function at home, school, and in social settings. ADHD is characterised by symptoms of inattention, hyperactivity, and impulsivity. Conduct disorder involves patterns of aggressive or antisocial behaviour, such as lying, stealing, and bullying. These disorders can lead to difficulties in academic and social settings.

Eating Disorders

Eating disorders, including anorexia nervosa, bulimia nervosa, and binge-eating disorder, are serious mental health conditions that affect young people. These disorders involve unhealthy eating behaviours and preoccupation with body image, which can lead to severe physical and psychological consequences. Symptoms may include extreme weight loss, binge eating, purging, and excessive exercise.

Self-Harm and Suicidal Behaviour

Self-harm and suicidal behaviour are critical concerns among young people. Self-harm involves intentionally injuring oneself, often as a way to cope with emotional pain. Suicidal behaviour includes thoughts of suicide, suicide attempts, and completed suicide. It is essential to take any signs of self-harm or suicidal behaviour seriously and seek immediate support.

Supporting Youth Mental Health

Supporting the mental health of young people requires a comprehensive approach that includes education, early intervention, access to mental health services, and creating a supportive environment.

Education and Awareness

Increasing education and awareness about mental health is crucial for reducing stigma and encouraging help-seeking behaviour. Schools, families, and communities can play a key role in providing information about mental health conditions, signs and symptoms, and available resources. Promoting open conversations about mental health can help young people feel more comfortable discussing their experiences and seeking support.

Early Intervention

Early intervention is essential for preventing mental health conditions from worsening and improving long-term outcomes. Identifying signs of mental health issues early and providing appropriate support can make a significant difference. This includes training teachers, parents, and healthcare providers to recognise the signs of mental health problems and knowing how to respond effectively.

Access to Mental Health Services

Ensuring young people have access to mental health services is crucial for addressing their needs. This includes providing school-based mental health services, community clinics, and online resources. Reducing barriers to access, such as cost, transportation, and stigma, can help more young people receive the support they need.

Creating a Supportive Environment

Creating a supportive environment involves fostering positive relationships, promoting resilience, and providing opportunities for young people to thrive. Families, schools, and communities can work together to create an environment that supports mental health.

Family Support

Families play a vital role in supporting youth mental health. Encouraging open communication, providing emotional support, and modelling healthy coping strategies can help young people feel secure and understood. Families can also seek professional help if needed and advocate for their child's mental health needs.

School Support

Schools can support mental health by creating a positive and inclusive environment. This includes implementing anti-bullying policies, promoting social-emotional learning, and providing access to counselling services. Schools can also offer programs that teach resilience, stress management, and healthy coping skills.

Community Support

Communities can support youth mental health by offering programs and resources that promote well-being. This includes recreational activities, mentorship programs, and access to mental health services. Creating safe and supportive spaces for young people to connect and seek help is essential for fostering a sense of belonging.

Conclusion

Youth mental health is a critical issue that requires attention and action from families, schools, communities, and policymakers. Understanding the unique challenges faced by young people and providing comprehensive support can promote positive mental health outcomes. By increasing education and awareness, ensuring access to mental health services, and creating supportive environments, we can help young people navigate the complexities of adolescence and young adulthood with resilience and confidence. Supporting youth mental health is not only essential for their well-being but also for the future health and prosperity of society as a whole.

CHAPTER 8: MENTAL HEALTH AND THE ELDERLY

Introduction

Mental health issues among the elderly are often overlooked, yet they are a significant concern that affects quality of life and overall well-being. As the global population ages, it becomes increasingly important to address the mental health needs of older adults. This chapter explores the mental health challenges faced by the elderly, the factors contributing to these challenges, and strategies for promoting mental well-being in later life.

The Prevalence of Mental Health Issues in the Elderly

Mental health conditions, such as depression, anxiety, and cognitive disorders, are common among older adults. According to the World Health Organization, approximately 15% of adults aged 60 and over suffer from a mental disorder. However, mental health issues in this demographic are frequently underdiagnosed and undertreated, partly due to the misconception that these problems are a normal part of ageing.

Factors Contributing to Mental Health Issues in the Elderly

Several factors contribute to the mental health challenges experienced by older adults. These include biological, psychological, social, and environmental influences.

Biological Factors

Biological factors, such as chronic health conditions and changes in brain chemistry, can significantly impact mental health in the elderly. Conditions like heart disease, diabetes, and arthritis can lead to chronic pain and disability, contributing to depression and anxiety. Additionally, neurodegenerative diseases, such as Alzheimer's and Parkinson's, can lead to cognitive decline and emotional distress.

Psychological Factors

Psychological factors, including coping mechanisms and personality traits, influence how older adults manage stress and life changes. Loss of independence, fear of mortality, and adjustment to retirement can lead to feelings of helplessness and depression. Developing healthy coping strategies is essential for managing these psychological stressors.

Social Factors

Social factors, such as isolation, loneliness, and loss of social support, play a critical role in the mental health of the elderly. As people age, they may experience the loss of loved ones, reduced social interactions, and changes in living arrangements. These social changes can lead to feelings of loneliness and social isolation, which are significant risk factors for mental health issues.

providing comprehensive support can promote positive mental health outcomes. By increasing education and awareness, ensuring access to mental health services, and creating supportive environments, we can help young people navigate the complexities of adolescence and young adulthood with resilience and confidence. Supporting youth mental health is not only essential for their well-being but also for the future health and prosperity of society as a whole.

CHAPTER 8: MENTAL HEALTH AND THE ELDERLY

Introduction

Mental health issues among the elderly are often overlooked, yet they are a significant concern that affects quality of life and overall well-being. As the global population ages, it becomes increasingly important to address the mental health needs of older adults. This chapter explores the mental health challenges faced by the elderly, the factors contributing to these challenges, and strategies for promoting mental well-being in later life.

The Prevalence of Mental Health Issues in the Elderly

Mental health conditions, such as depression, anxiety, and cognitive disorders, are common among older adults. According to the World Health Organization, approximately 15% of adults aged 60 and over suffer from a mental disorder. However, mental health issues in this demographic are frequently underdiagnosed and undertreated, partly due to the misconception that these problems are a normal part of ageing.

Factors Contributing to Mental Health Issues in the Elderly

Several factors contribute to the mental health challenges experienced by older adults. These include biological, psychological, social, and environmental influences.

Biological Factors

Biological factors, such as chronic health conditions and changes in brain chemistry, can significantly impact mental health in the elderly. Conditions like heart disease, diabetes, and arthritis can lead to chronic pain and disability, contributing to depression and anxiety. Additionally, neurodegenerative diseases, such as Alzheimer's and Parkinson's, can lead to cognitive decline and emotional distress.

Psychological Factors

Psychological factors, including coping mechanisms and personality traits, influence how older adults manage stress and life changes. Loss of independence, fear of mortality, and adjustment to retirement can lead to feelings of helplessness and depression. Developing healthy coping strategies is essential for managing these psychological stressors.

Social Factors

Social factors, such as isolation, loneliness, and loss of social support, play a critical role in the mental health of the elderly. As people age, they may experience the loss of loved ones, reduced social interactions, and changes in living arrangements. These social changes can lead to feelings of loneliness and social isolation, which are significant risk factors for mental health issues.

Environmental Factors

Environmental factors, including living conditions and access to healthcare, influence mental health in older adults. Poor living conditions, such as inadequate housing or unsafe neighbourhoods, can exacerbate stress and anxiety. Additionally, barriers to accessing mental health services, such as transportation difficulties and financial constraints, can prevent older adults from receiving the care they need.

Common Mental Health Issues Among the Elderly

Older adults can experience a range of mental health issues, each with unique symptoms and challenges. Understanding these conditions is crucial for providing appropriate support and intervention.

Depression

Depression is one of the most common mental health issues in the elderly. It is characterised by persistent sadness, lack of interest in activities, changes in appetite and sleep patterns, fatigue, and feelings of hopelessness. Depression in older adults is often linked to physical health problems, loss of loved ones, and social isolation. It is essential to differentiate between depression and normal grief to provide effective treatment.

Anxiety

Anxiety disorders, including generalised anxiety disorder, panic disorder, and phobias, can significantly impact the quality of life of older adults. Symptoms may include excessive worry, restlessness, muscle tension, and difficulty sleeping. Anxiety in the elderly can be triggered by health concerns, financial stress, and changes in living situations.

Cognitive Disorders

Cognitive disorders, such as dementia and mild cognitive impairment, affect memory, thinking, and behaviour. Alzheimer's disease is the most common form of dementia, characterised by progressive memory loss, confusion, and changes in mood and behaviour. Cognitive disorders can lead to significant emotional distress for both the affected individuals and their caregivers.

Substance Abuse

Substance abuse is an often-overlooked issue among older adults. Some may misuse alcohol, prescription medications, or other substances to cope with pain, sleep problems, or emotional distress. Substance abuse can exacerbate mental health issues and lead to a decline in physical health and social functioning.

Supporting Mental Health in the Elderly

Supporting the mental health of older adults requires a comprehensive approach that includes education, early intervention, access to mental health services, and creating a supportive environment.

Education and Awareness

Increasing education and awareness about mental health in older adults is crucial for reducing stigma and encouraging help-seeking behaviour. Families, caregivers, and healthcare providers can play a key role in providing information about mental health conditions, signs and symptoms, and available resources. Promoting open conversations about mental health can help older adults feel more comfortable discussing their experiences and seeking support.

Early Intervention

Early intervention is essential for preventing mental health conditions from worsening and improving long-term outcomes. Identifying signs of mental health issues early and providing appropriate support can make a significant difference. This includes training healthcare providers to recognise the signs of mental health problems and knowing how to respond effectively.

Access to Mental Health Services

Ensuring older adults have access to mental health services is crucial for addressing their needs. This includes providing community-based mental health services, integrating mental health care into primary care, and offering telehealth options. Reducing barriers to access, such as cost, transportation, and stigma, can help more older adults receive the support they need.

Creating a Supportive Environment

Creating a supportive environment involves fostering positive relationships, promoting resilience, and providing opportunities for older adults to thrive. Families, communities, and healthcare systems can work together to create an environment that supports mental health.

Family Support

Families play a vital role in supporting the mental health of older adults. Encouraging open communication, providing emotional support, and involving older adults in family activities can help them feel valued and connected. Families can also seek professional help if needed and advocate for their loved one's mental health needs.

Community Support

Communities can support the mental health of older adults by offering programs and resources that promote well-being. This includes recreational activities, social clubs, volunteer opportunities, and access to mental health services. Creating safe and supportive spaces for older adults to connect and seek help is essential for fostering a sense of belonging.

Healthcare Support

Healthcare providers can support mental health by integrating mental health screenings and care into routine medical visits. This includes providing training on geriatric mental health, offering counselling and therapy services, and coordinating care with mental health specialists. Ensuring that mental health is a regular part of healthcare for older adults can improve early detection and treatment.

The Role of Technology

Technology can play a significant role in supporting the mental health of older adults. Digital tools and platforms can provide access to mental health resources, facilitate social connections, and offer opportunities for engagement and learning.

Telehealth Services

Telehealth services can increase access to mental health care for older adults, especially those with mobility issues or living in remote areas. Virtual consultations with mental health professionals can provide support and treatment without the need for travel.

Online Communities

Online communities and social media platforms can help older adults stay connected with family and friends, reducing feelings of loneliness and isolation. These platforms can also provide access to support groups and mental health resources.

Mental Health Apps

Mental health apps can offer tools for managing stress, anxiety, and depression. These apps can provide guided meditation, cognitive-behavioural therapy exercises, and mood tracking. Ensuring that these tools are user-friendly for older adults is important for their effectiveness.

Conclusion

Mental health in the elderly is a critical issue that requires attention and action from families, communities, healthcare providers, and policymakers. Understanding the unique challenges faced by older adults and providing comprehensive support can promote positive mental health outcomes. By increasing education and awareness, ensuring access to mental health services, creating supportive environments, and leveraging technology, we can help older adults maintain their mental well-being. Supporting the mental health of the elderly is not only essential for their quality of life but also for the overall health and well-being of our society.

CHAPTER 9: THE IMPORTANCE OF SUPPORT SYSTEMS

Introduction

Support systems play a crucial role in maintaining and improving mental health. Whether they consist of family, friends, professionals, or community resources, these networks provide emotional, practical, and sometimes even financial support that is essential for well-being. This chapter explores the different types of support systems, their importance in mental health, and how to build and maintain these networks effectively.

Understanding Support Systems

Support systems can be broadly categorised into three types: emotional support, informational support, and practical support. Each type plays a unique role in promoting mental health and helping individuals navigate life's challenges.

Emotional Support

Emotional support involves expressions of empathy, love, trust, and care. It provides individuals with the comfort and reassurance they need to feel understood and valued. This type of support can come from family members, friends, romantic partners, and even pets. It helps individuals cope with stress, boosts self-esteem, and fosters a sense of belonging.

Informational Support

Informational support includes advice, suggestions, and information that helps individuals solve problems and make decisions. This support can come from professionals, such as therapists and counsellors, as well as from knowledgeable friends and family members. Access to accurate and timely information is critical for managing mental health conditions and navigating complex life situations.

Practical Support

Practical support, also known as instrumental support, involves tangible help with daily tasks and responsibilities. This can include financial assistance, help with chores, transportation, and childcare. Practical support alleviates the burden of daily life, allowing individuals to focus on their mental health and recovery.

The Role of Family in Support Systems

Family is often the cornerstone of an individual's support system. Family members provide consistent emotional and practical support, which is crucial for mental health. However, the effectiveness of family support can vary based on family dynamics, communication patterns, and the presence of any existing mental health issues within the family.

Emotional Bonds and Mental Health

Strong emotional bonds within a family can significantly enhance mental health. Families that express love, care, and understanding create a safe environment where individuals feel valued and supported. Open communication and mutual respect are essential for maintaining these bonds and providing effective support.

ensuring access to mental health services, creating supportive environments, and leveraging technology, we can help older adults maintain their mental well-being. Supporting the mental health of the elderly is not only essential for their quality of life but also for the overall health and well-being of our society.

CHAPTER 9: THE IMPORTANCE OF SUPPORT SYSTEMS

Introduction

Support systems play a crucial role in maintaining and improving mental health. Whether they consist of family, friends, professionals, or community resources, these networks provide emotional, practical, and sometimes even financial support that is essential for well-being. This chapter explores the different types of support systems, their importance in mental health, and how to build and maintain these networks effectively.

Understanding Support Systems

Support systems can be broadly categorised into three types: emotional support, informational support, and practical support. Each type plays a unique role in promoting mental health and helping individuals navigate life's challenges.

Emotional Support

Emotional support involves expressions of empathy, love, trust, and care. It provides individuals with the comfort and reassurance they need to feel understood and valued. This type of support can come from family members, friends, romantic partners, and even pets. It helps individuals cope with stress, boosts self-esteem, and fosters a sense of belonging.

Informational Support

Informational support includes advice, suggestions, and information that helps individuals solve problems and make decisions. This support can come from professionals, such as therapists and counsellors, as well as from knowledgeable friends and family members. Access to accurate and timely information is critical for managing mental health conditions and navigating complex life situations.

Practical Support

Practical support, also known as instrumental support, involves tangible help with daily tasks and responsibilities. This can include financial assistance, help with chores, transportation, and childcare. Practical support alleviates the burden of daily life, allowing individuals to focus on their mental health and recovery.

The Role of Family in Support Systems

Family is often the cornerstone of an individual's support system. Family members provide consistent emotional and practical support, which is crucial for mental health. However, the effectiveness of family support can vary based on family dynamics, communication patterns, and the presence of any existing mental health issues within the family.

Emotional Bonds and Mental Health

Strong emotional bonds within a family can significantly enhance mental health. Families that express love, care, and understanding create a safe environment where individuals feel valued and supported. Open communication and mutual respect are essential for maintaining these bonds and providing effective support.

Practical Assistance

Family members often step in to provide practical assistance during times of need. This can include help with household tasks, financial support, and caregiving. Such assistance can relieve stress and allow individuals to focus on their mental health and well-being.

Challenges in Family Support

While family support is invaluable, it can also present challenges. Family members may not always understand the complexities of mental health conditions, leading to misunderstandings and conflicts. Additionally, some families may have strained relationships that hinder effective support. In such cases, seeking external help, such as family therapy, can be beneficial.

Friends as a Support System

Friends play a crucial role in providing emotional and social support. Friendships offer companionship, shared experiences, and a sense of belonging, all of which are vital for mental health.

Emotional Support from Friends

Friends provide a unique form of emotional support that complements family support. They offer a different perspective, shared interests, and a break from family dynamics. Friends can provide a listening ear, offer encouragement, and help individuals feel less isolated.

Social Interaction and Mental Health

Social interaction is essential for mental health. Friendships provide opportunities for socialising, which can reduce feelings of loneliness and depression. Engaging in social activities with friends can also help individuals manage stress and improve their overall mood.

Building and Maintaining Friendships

Building and maintaining friendships requires effort and mutual understanding. It is important to nurture these relationships through regular communication, spending quality time together, and supporting each other during difficult times. Healthy friendships are built on trust, respect, and reciprocity.

Professional Support Systems

Professional support systems, including therapists, counsellors, and mental health professionals, play a critical role in managing mental health conditions. These professionals provide specialised care and support that is essential for recovery and well-being.

Therapy and Counselling

Therapists and counsellors offer a safe and confidential space for individuals to explore their thoughts and feelings. They use evidence-based techniques to help individuals manage symptoms, develop coping strategies, and improve their mental health. Regular therapy sessions can provide ongoing support and guidance.

Medical Support

Psychiatrists and other medical professionals provide essential medical support for individuals with mental health conditions. This can include diagnosis, medication management, and treatment planning. Medical support is crucial for individuals with conditions that require pharmacological intervention.

Support Groups

Support groups offer a unique form of peer support where individuals with similar experiences can share their stories and provide mutual encouragement. These groups can be particularly beneficial for individuals with specific mental health conditions, as they provide a sense of community and understanding.

Community and Organisational Support

Community resources and organisations play an important role in supporting mental health. These can include community centres, religious organisations, non-profits, and online communities.

Community Centres and Non-Profits

Community centres and non-profit organisations often offer mental health programs, workshops, and resources. These services can include counselling, support groups, educational materials, and recreational activities that promote well-being.

Religious and Spiritual Support

For many individuals, religious and spiritual organisations provide significant support. These organisations offer a sense of community, moral guidance, and opportunities for social interaction. Many religious institutions also provide pastoral counselling and support groups.

Online Communities

Online communities offer a convenient and accessible form of support, especially for those who may have difficulty accessing traditional support systems. Online forums, social media groups, and virtual support groups allow individuals to connect with others, share experiences, and access resources.

Building and Strengthening Support Systems

Building and strengthening support systems is essential for maintaining mental health. This involves actively seeking and nurturing relationships, being open to receiving support, and giving support in return.

Seeking Support

Seeking support requires recognising the need for help and reaching out to others. This can involve talking to family and friends, joining support groups, or seeking professional help. It is important to overcome the stigma associated with seeking help and understand that everyone needs support at times.

Nurturing Relationships

Nurturing relationships involves regular communication, showing appreciation, and being there for others. Building strong, healthy relationships requires effort and mutual respect. It is important to invest time and energy into maintaining these connections.

Providing Support

Providing support to others can be equally beneficial for mental health. Helping others can create a sense of purpose, build social connections, and improve self-esteem. Being a supportive friend or family member can strengthen relationships and create a supportive network.

Conclusion

Support systems are a vital component of mental health. They provide the emotional, informational, and practical support necessary to navigate life's challenges and maintain well-being. Understanding the different types of support systems and their importance can help individuals build and strengthen these networks. By seeking support, nurturing relationships, and providing support to others, we can create a community that promotes mental health and well-being for all.

CHAPTER 10: THERAPEUTIC APPROACHES TO MENTAL HEALTH

Introduction

Therapeutic approaches to mental health encompass a wide range of treatments and techniques designed to help individuals manage and overcome mental health challenges. These approaches are tailored to address the unique needs of each individual, taking into consideration their specific condition, personal history, and preferences. This chapter explores various therapeutic modalities, their principles, and their applications in promoting mental well-being.

Psychotherapy

Psychotherapy, also known as talk therapy, involves working with a trained therapist to explore thoughts, feelings, and behaviours. It aims to help individuals understand their issues, develop coping strategies, and make positive changes in their lives. There are several forms of psychotherapy, each with its own theoretical foundation and techniques.

Cognitive Behavioural Therapy (CBT)

Cognitive Behavioural Therapy (CBT) is one of the most widely used and researched forms of psychotherapy. It focuses on identifying and changing negative thought patterns and behaviours that contribute to mental health problems. CBT is structured, goal-oriented, and typically short-term.

Principles of CBT:

- Thoughts, feelings, and behaviours are interconnected.

- Negative thoughts and behaviours can be changed to improve mental health.

- Individuals can learn to identify and challenge cognitive distortions.

Applications:

CBT is effective for a range of conditions, including depression, anxiety disorders, phobias, and post-traumatic stress disorder (PTSD). It involves techniques such as cognitive restructuring, behavioural activation, and exposure therapy.

Dialectical Behaviour Therapy (DBT)

Dialectical Behaviour Therapy (DBT) is a form of cognitive-behavioural therapy that emphasises the balance between acceptance and change. It was originally developed for individuals with borderline personality disorder but has since been adapted for other conditions.

Principles of DBT:

- Validation and acceptance of the individual's experiences.

- Skills training in areas such as emotional regulation, distress tolerance, interpersonal effectiveness, and mindfulness.

- Balancing acceptance of the present with efforts to change.

Applications:

DBT is particularly effective for borderline personality disorder, self-harming behaviours, and chronic suicidal ideation. It involves individual therapy, group skills training, and phone coaching.

Psychodynamic Therapy

Psychodynamic therapy is based on the theories of Sigmund Freud and focuses on understanding the unconscious mind and its influence on behaviour. It involves exploring past experiences, unresolved conflicts, and patterns of behaviour that affect current functioning.

Principles of Psychodynamic Therapy:

- Unconscious processes influence behaviour and emotions.

- Early life experiences shape personality and current issues.

- Insight into unconscious conflicts can lead to emotional growth and symptom relief.

Applications:

Psychodynamic therapy is used for a variety of mental health conditions, including depression, anxiety, and personality disorders. It is typically longer-term and involves exploring childhood experiences, dreams, and fantasies.

Humanistic Therapy

Humanistic therapy, including approaches like Person-Centred Therapy and Gestalt Therapy, emphasises the individual's capacity for self-awareness and personal growth. It focuses on the present moment and the individual's experience.

Principles of Humanistic Therapy:

- Emphasis on personal responsibility and self-actualisation.

- The therapist provides a non-judgmental, empathetic, and accepting environment.

- Focus on the individual's subjective experience and inherent potential for growth.

Applications:

Humanistic therapy is effective for enhancing self-esteem, improving relationships, and fostering personal growth. It is used for a range of issues, including depression, anxiety, and life transitions.

Behavioural Therapies

Behavioural therapies focus on modifying unhealthy behaviours through various techniques. These approaches are often used in combination with cognitive therapies.

Exposure Therapy

Exposure therapy is a behavioural technique used to treat anxiety disorders, particularly phobias, PTSD, and obsessive-compulsive disorder (OCD). It involves gradually exposing the individual to feared objects or situations in a controlled manner to reduce fear and avoidance.

Principles of Exposure Therapy:

- Gradual exposure to feared stimuli reduces anxiety over time.

- The individual learns that feared consequences are unlikely to occur.

- Repeated exposure leads to desensitisation and decreased fear.

Applications:

Exposure therapy is effective for treating specific phobias, social anxiety, PTSD, and OCD. Techniques include in vivo exposure (real-life exposure), imaginal exposure (visualising feared situations), and interoceptive exposure (exposure to physical sensations of anxiety).

Behavioural Activation

Behavioural activation is a technique used primarily to treat depression. It involves encouraging individuals to engage in activities that are likely to improve their mood and decrease depressive symptoms.

Principles of Behavioural Activation:

- Depression often leads to withdrawal from activities that provide pleasure and a sense of accomplishment.

- Increasing engagement in positive activities can improve mood and reduce depressive symptoms.

- Activity scheduling and goal-setting are key components.

Applications:

Behavioural activation is effective for treating depression and can be used in both individual and group therapy settings. It involves identifying values, setting goals, and planning activities that align with those values.

Integrative and Holistic Therapies

Integrative and holistic therapies consider the whole person, including their physical, emotional, mental, and spiritual well-being. These approaches often combine elements of different therapeutic modalities.

Mindfulness-Based Therapies

Mindfulness-based therapies, such as Mindfulness-Based Stress Reduction (MBSR) and Mindfulness-Based Cognitive Therapy (MBCT), incorporate mindfulness practices to help individuals manage stress and improve mental health.

Principles of Mindfulness-Based Therapies:

- Mindfulness involves paying attention to the present moment non-judgmentally.

- Developing mindfulness skills can reduce stress, anxiety, and depression.

- Regular practice of mindfulness meditation is central to these therapies.

Applications:

Mindfulness-based therapies are effective for a range of conditions, including depression, anxiety, chronic pain, and stress-related disorders. They involve mindfulness meditation, body scanning, and mindful movement.

Art and Music Therapy

Art and music therapy use creative processes to help individuals express themselves and explore their emotions. These therapies provide a non-verbal outlet for processing experiences and can be particularly beneficial for those who find it difficult to articulate their feelings.

Principles of Art and Music Therapy:

- Creative expression can facilitate emotional release and insight.

- The process of creating art or music is therapeutic in itself.

- These therapies can enhance self-awareness and self-esteem.

Applications:

Art and music therapy are used for a variety of conditions, including trauma, depression, anxiety, and developmental disorders. They involve activities such as painting, drawing, playing instruments, and composing music.

Medication and Biological Treatments

Medication and other biological treatments are often used in conjunction with psychotherapy to manage mental health conditions. These treatments address the biological aspects of mental health disorders.

Psychopharmacology

Psychopharmacology involves the use of medications to manage mental health conditions. Different classes of medications target specific symptoms and neurochemical imbalances.

Common Medications:

- Antidepressants: Used to treat depression and anxiety disorders.

- Antipsychotics: Used to treat schizophrenia and bipolar disorder.

- Mood stabilisers: Used to treat bipolar disorder.

- Anxiolytics: Used to treat anxiety disorders.

- Stimulants: Used to treat attention-deficit/hyperactivity disorder (ADHD).

Applications:

Medications can be essential for managing severe or chronic mental health conditions. They are often used in combination with psychotherapy for comprehensive treatment.

Electroconvulsive Therapy (ECT)

Electroconvulsive therapy (ECT) is a medical treatment that involves inducing controlled seizures to provide relief from severe mental health conditions.

Principles of ECT:

- ECT is typically used when other treatments have been ineffective.

- It is administered under general anaesthesia and involves electrical stimulation of the brain.

- ECT can provide rapid relief from severe symptoms.

Applications:

ECT is primarily used for severe depression, treatment-resistant depression, bipolar disorder, and severe psychosis. It is often considered when there is an urgent need for treatment, such as in cases of suicidal ideation.

Alternative and Complementary Therapies

Alternative and complementary therapies include a variety of treatments that are used alongside or instead of conventional medical treatments. These approaches focus on holistic well-being and often incorporate lifestyle changes.

Acupuncture

Acupuncture is a traditional Chinese medicine practice that involves inserting thin needles into specific points on the body to promote healing and balance.

Principles of Acupuncture:

- It is based on the concept of energy flow (Qi) and meridians in the body.

- Acupuncture aims to restore balance and alleviate symptoms.

- It can influence the nervous system and release endorphins.

Applications:

Acupuncture is used for a variety of conditions, including anxiety, depression, chronic pain, and stress. It is often used as a complementary treatment to enhance overall well-being.

Herbal and Nutritional Supplements

Herbal and nutritional supplements are used to support mental health and address specific symptoms. These supplements can include vitamins, minerals, and herbal extracts.

Common Supplements:

- St. John's Wort: Used for mild to moderate depression.

- Omega-3 fatty acids: Used for depression and bipolar disorder.

- Valerian root: Used for anxiety and insomnia.

- Magnesium: Used for anxiety and mood regulation.

Applications:

Supplements can provide additional support for mental health when used appropriately. It is important to consult with a healthcare provider before starting any supplements to ensure safety and effectiveness.

Conclusion

Therapeutic approaches to mental health are diverse and adaptable, offering a range of options to meet the unique needs of each individual. From psychotherapy and behavioural therapies to medication and alternative treatments, these approaches provide comprehensive care for mental health conditions. Understanding the principles and applications of various therapies can help individuals make informed decisions about their mental health care and find the support they need to achieve well-being.

CHAPTER 11: THE ROLE OF POLICY IN MENTAL HEALTH ADVOCACY

Introduction

Policy plays a crucial role in shaping the landscape of mental health advocacy. Effective mental health policies can provide a framework for ensuring that individuals receive the care and support they need, while also promoting awareness and reducing stigma. This chapter explores the importance of mental health policies, key components of effective policies, and how advocacy efforts can influence policy change to improve mental health outcomes.

The Importance of Mental Health Policies

Mental health policies are essential for several reasons. They provide a structured approach to addressing mental health issues at a systemic level, ensuring that mental health services are accessible, equitable, and of high quality. Policies also help to allocate resources, establish standards of care, and promote research and education.

Accessibility and Equity

One of the primary goals of mental health policy is to ensure that all individuals have access to mental health services regardless of their socio-economic status, geographical location, or other barriers. Policies can mandate the provision of services in underserved areas, ensure that insurance covers mental health treatment, and promote the integration of mental health care into primary health care settings.

Quality and Standards of Care

Mental health policies establish standards of care that ensure services are safe, effective, and patient-centred. These standards may include guidelines for treatment protocols, training requirements for mental health professionals, and measures for monitoring and evaluating service delivery. By setting these standards, policies help to maintain high-quality care across various service providers.

Funding and Resource Allocation

Effective mental health policies are essential for securing and allocating funding for mental health services. This includes funding for public mental health services, community programs, research initiatives, and education campaigns. Adequate funding is critical to ensuring that mental health services can meet the needs of the population.

Key Components of Effective Mental Health Policies

Effective mental health policies typically include several key components that address the various aspects of mental health care and support. These components help to create a comprehensive approach to mental health advocacy and service provision.

Comprehensive Service Provision

An effective mental health policy ensures that a wide range of services is available to meet the diverse needs of individuals with mental health conditions. This includes preventative services, early intervention, crisis intervention, inpatient and outpatient care, and rehabilitation services. Policies should also promote the integration of mental health services with other health and social services.

Promotion of Mental Health and Prevention of Mental Disorders

Policies should include strategies for promoting mental health and preventing mental disorders. This can involve public awareness campaigns, educational programs, and initiatives aimed at reducing risk factors such as substance abuse, domestic violence, and socio-economic disparities. By focusing on prevention, policies can help reduce the incidence and impact of mental health conditions.

Protection of Human Rights

Mental health policies must protect the human rights of individuals with mental health conditions. This includes ensuring that individuals receive care with dignity and respect, protecting against discrimination and abuse, and promoting autonomy and informed consent. Policies should also support the rights of individuals to participate in their own care and in decisions that affect their lives.

Training and Workforce Development

An effective mental health policy includes provisions for the training and development of the mental health workforce. This ensures that mental health professionals are well-equipped to provide high-quality care and support. Policies should promote ongoing education and training, certification and licensing requirements, and measures to address workforce shortages.

The Role of Advocacy in Influencing Policy Change

Advocacy efforts are crucial in shaping and influencing mental health policy. Advocates work to raise awareness, mobilise public support, and engage with policymakers to bring about positive changes in mental health legislation and funding.

Raising Awareness and Reducing Stigma

Advocacy campaigns play a vital role in raising awareness about mental health issues and reducing stigma. By educating the public and promoting positive messages about mental health, advocates can create a more supportive and understanding environment. This, in turn, can influence policymakers to prioritise mental health issues and support relevant policy changes.

Engaging with Policymakers

Advocates often engage directly with policymakers to promote changes in mental health policy. This can involve lobbying efforts, providing testimony at legislative hearings, and participating in policy advisory committees. By presenting evidence-based arguments and highlighting the experiences of individuals with mental health conditions, advocates can influence policymakers to adopt more effective and inclusive mental health policies.

Mobilising Public Support

Public support is a powerful tool in influencing policy change. Advocacy groups often mobilise public support through campaigns, petitions, and social media. By demonstrating widespread public concern and support for mental health issues, advocates can pressure policymakers to take action and prioritise mental health in their agendas.

Building Coalitions and Partnerships

Collaboration is key to effective advocacy. Building coalitions and partnerships with other advocacy groups, non-profit organisations, healthcare providers, and community leaders can amplify advocacy efforts and create a stronger, unified voice for mental health. These partnerships can also provide additional resources and expertise to support advocacy initiatives.

Case Studies in Policy and Advocacy

Examining case studies of successful mental health policy initiatives can provide valuable insights into the role of advocacy in influencing policy change. Here are a few examples of effective advocacy and policy initiatives:

The Mental Health Parity and Addiction Equity Act (MHPAEA) in the United States

The MHPAEA, passed in 2008, is a significant piece of legislation that requires health insurance plans to provide equal coverage for mental health and substance use disorders as they do for physical health conditions. Advocacy efforts played a crucial role in the passage of this act, with mental health advocates, patient groups, and healthcare providers working together to raise awareness and push for legislative change.

The Mental Health Act in the United Kingdom

The Mental Health Act 1983, and its subsequent amendments, provide a legal framework for the treatment and care of individuals with mental health conditions in the UK. Advocacy groups have been instrumental in influencing amendments to the act, ensuring that it protects the rights of individuals with mental health conditions and promotes access to high-quality care. Ongoing advocacy efforts continue to push for further reforms to improve the act.

The National Mental Health Strategy in Australia

Australia's National Mental Health Strategy outlines a framework for promoting mental health and improving mental health services across the country. The strategy has been shaped by extensive consultation with mental health advocates, service providers, and individuals with lived experience. Advocacy efforts have been key in ensuring that the strategy addresses the needs of diverse populations and promotes equitable access to care.

Challenges and Opportunities in Mental Health Policy

While significant progress has been made in mental health policy, several challenges remain. Addressing these challenges presents opportunities for further advocacy and policy development.

Overcoming Stigma and Discrimination

Despite advances in mental health awareness, stigma and discrimination remain significant barriers to effective mental health policy. Advocacy efforts must continue to focus on reducing stigma and promoting understanding and acceptance of mental health conditions.

Ensuring Adequate Funding

Securing adequate funding for mental health services is an ongoing challenge. Advocates must work to ensure that mental health is prioritised in government budgets and that funding is allocated to areas of greatest need. This includes advocating for funding for research, education, and community-based services.

Addressing Health Disparities

Health disparities, including those based on socio-economic status, race, ethnicity, and geographical location, can impact access to mental health services. Effective policies must address these disparities and promote equity in mental health care. Advocacy efforts should focus on highlighting these disparities and pushing for policy changes that promote inclusivity and equity.

Conclusion

Mental health policies play a critical role in shaping the mental health landscape and ensuring that individuals receive the care and support they need. Effective policies promote accessibility, quality, and equity in mental health services, and are influenced by robust advocacy efforts. By raising awareness, engaging with policymakers, and mobilising public support, advocates can drive positive changes in mental health policy. Continued efforts are needed to overcome challenges and seize opportunities to improve mental health outcomes for all individuals.

CHAPTER 12: COMMUNITY-BASED MENTAL HEALTH PROGRAMS

Introduction

Community-based mental health programs play a pivotal role in providing accessible, localised, and holistic support to individuals with mental health conditions. These programs are designed to address the unique needs of communities, fostering environments where mental health can be supported through a network of services, resources, and social connections. This chapter explores the importance of community-based mental health programs, various types of programs, their benefits, and the challenges they face.

The Importance of Community-Based Mental Health Programs

Community-based mental health programs are essential for several reasons. They offer localised care that is often more accessible and tailored to the specific needs of the community. These programs also provide a holistic approach to mental health, integrating services and supports that address the social determinants of health.

Accessibility and Localisation

One of the main advantages of community-based programs is their accessibility. These programs are often located within the community they serve, making it easier for individuals to access services without the need for long travel or extensive waiting times. Localised care ensures that services are culturally appropriate and responsive to the specific needs of the community.

Holistic Approach

Community-based mental health programs adopt a holistic approach to mental health care. They consider the broad range of factors that impact mental health, including social, economic, and environmental factors. By addressing these determinants, community-based programs can provide more comprehensive support that goes beyond just treating symptoms.

Types of Community-Based Mental Health Programs

Community-based mental health programs can take many forms, each designed to address different aspects of mental health and well-being. Some of the common types of programs include community mental health centres, peer support groups, crisis intervention services, and outreach programs.

Community Mental Health Centres

Community mental health centres provide a wide range of services, including assessment, counselling, therapy, and psychiatric care. These centres often serve as a hub for mental health services in the community, offering a central location where individuals can access comprehensive care.

Services Provided:

- Individual and group therapy

- Medication management

- Case management and care coordination

- Psychoeducation and support groups

- Crisis intervention

Benefits:

Community mental health centres offer a one-stop-shop for mental health services, making it easier for individuals to receive coordinated and continuous care. They also provide opportunities for collaboration among different service providers, ensuring a more integrated approach to mental health care.

Peer Support Groups

Peer support groups are an invaluable component of community-based mental health programs. These groups are facilitated by individuals who have lived experience with mental health conditions, providing a supportive environment where participants can share their experiences, challenges, and successes.

Benefits:

- Reducing feelings of isolation and loneliness

- Providing a sense of community and belonging

- Offering practical advice and coping strategies

- Empowering individuals through shared experiences

Examples:

Peer support groups can be found in various settings, including community centres, hospitals, and online platforms. They may focus on specific mental health conditions, such as depression or anxiety, or broader topics like addiction recovery or trauma support.

Crisis Intervention Services

Crisis intervention services provide immediate support to individuals experiencing a mental health crisis. These services aim to stabilise the individual, provide short-term care, and connect them with ongoing support and resources.

Components of Crisis Intervention:

- 24/7 crisis hotlines

- Mobile crisis teams

- Crisis stabilisation units

- Emergency department partnerships

Benefits:

Crisis intervention services can prevent hospitalisation and reduce the burden on emergency services by providing timely and appropriate care in the community. They also ensure that individuals receive support during critical moments, which can be crucial for their safety and well-being.

Outreach Programs

Outreach programs aim to reach individuals who may not seek help through traditional channels. These programs often focus on vulnerable populations, such as the homeless, immigrants, and individuals in rural or remote areas.

Activities:

- Providing information and education about mental health

- Offering screening and referral services

- Distributing resources and support materials

- Building relationships with community members to encourage help-seeking

Benefits:

Outreach programs help to bridge gaps in service delivery, ensuring that all members of the community have access to mental health support. They also play a crucial role in raising awareness and reducing stigma around mental health issues.

Benefits of Community-Based Mental Health Programs

Community-based mental health programs offer numerous benefits, both for individuals and the broader community. These benefits include increased access to care, improved mental health outcomes, enhanced community resilience, and reduced stigma.

Increased Access to Care

By providing services within the community, these programs reduce barriers to accessing care. This is particularly important for individuals who may face challenges such as transportation issues, financial constraints, or stigma associated with seeking help.

Improved Mental Health Outcomes

Community-based programs offer timely and appropriate interventions that can lead to better mental health outcomes. Early intervention and continuous support help individuals manage their conditions more effectively, reducing the risk of relapse and hospitalisation.

Enhanced Community Resilience

These programs strengthen the community by fostering a supportive environment where individuals can thrive. By promoting mental health and well-being, community-based programs contribute to overall community resilience and social cohesion.

Reduced Stigma

Community-based programs play a vital role in reducing stigma by normalising conversations about mental health and providing visible and accessible support. By integrating mental health services into the fabric of the community, these programs help to create an environment where seeking help is seen as a normal and positive step.

Challenges Facing Community-Based Mental Health Programs

Despite their many benefits, community-based mental health programs face several challenges that can impact their effectiveness and sustainability. These challenges include funding limitations, workforce shortages, and the need for ongoing evaluation and improvement.

Funding Limitations

Securing adequate funding is a significant challenge for many community-based mental health programs. Limited financial resources can restrict the range of services offered, affect the quality of care, and limit the program's ability to reach all members of the community.

Workforce Shortages

There is often a shortage of trained mental health professionals available to work in community-based settings. This can lead to high caseloads, burnout among staff, and challenges in providing timely and effective care. Efforts to recruit, train, and retain mental health professionals are essential to addressing this issue.

Need for Ongoing Evaluation and Improvement

Continuous evaluation is necessary to ensure that community-based mental health programs are meeting the needs of the community and providing high-quality care. This includes collecting data on outcomes, seeking feedback from participants, and making adjustments based on evidence and best practices.

Conclusion

Community-based mental health programs are a cornerstone of effective mental health care, providing accessible, localised, and holistic support to individuals within their communities. These programs offer numerous benefits, including increased access to care, improved mental health outcomes, and reduced stigma. However, they also face challenges such as funding limitations and workforce shortages. Addressing these challenges and continuing to develop and support community-based programs is essential for promoting mental health and well-being for all individuals. Through collaboration, advocacy, and innovation, communities can build stronger, more resilient mental health support systems.

CHAPTER 13: GLOBAL PERSPECTIVES ON MENTAL HEALTH

Introduction

These programs strengthen the community by fostering a supportive environment where individuals can thrive. By promoting mental health and well-being, community-based programs contribute to overall community resilience and social cohesion.

Reduced Stigma

Community-based programs play a vital role in reducing stigma by normalising conversations about mental health and providing visible and accessible support. By integrating mental health services into the fabric of the community, these programs help to create an environment where seeking help is seen as a normal and positive step.

Challenges Facing Community-Based Mental Health Programs

Despite their many benefits, community-based mental health programs face several challenges that can impact their effectiveness and sustainability. These challenges include funding limitations, workforce shortages, and the need for ongoing evaluation and improvement.

Funding Limitations

Securing adequate funding is a significant challenge for many community-based mental health programs. Limited financial resources can restrict the range of services offered, affect the quality of care, and limit the program's ability to reach all members of the community.

Workforce Shortages

There is often a shortage of trained mental health professionals available to work in community-based settings. This can lead to high caseloads, burnout among staff, and challenges in providing timely and effective care. Efforts to recruit, train, and retain mental health professionals are essential to addressing this issue.

Need for Ongoing Evaluation and Improvement

Continuous evaluation is necessary to ensure that community-based mental health programs are meeting the needs of the community and providing high-quality care. This includes collecting data on outcomes, seeking feedback from participants, and making adjustments based on evidence and best practices.

Conclusion

Community-based mental health programs are a cornerstone of effective mental health care, providing accessible, localised, and holistic support to individuals within their communities. These programs offer numerous benefits, including increased access to care, improved mental health outcomes, and reduced stigma. However, they also face challenges such as funding limitations and workforce shortages. Addressing these challenges and continuing to develop and support community-based programs is essential for promoting mental health and well-being for all individuals. Through collaboration, advocacy, and innovation, communities can build stronger, more resilient mental health support systems.

CHAPTER 13: GLOBAL PERSPECTIVES ON MENTAL HEALTH

Introduction

Mental health is a universal concern, yet the way it is understood, addressed, and treated varies widely across different cultures and regions. This chapter explores the global perspectives on mental health, highlighting the diverse approaches, challenges, and innovations in mental health care around the world. Understanding these global perspectives provides valuable insights into how different societies handle mental health issues and can inspire new ways to improve mental health care universally.

Cultural Attitudes Towards Mental Health

Cultural attitudes play a significant role in shaping the understanding and treatment of mental health conditions. These attitudes influence everything from the stigma associated with mental illness to the types of treatments considered acceptable.

Western Perspectives

In many Western countries, mental health is often approached from a biomedical perspective. Conditions such as depression, anxiety, and schizophrenia are typically understood as medical issues that require clinical intervention. Psychotherapy, medication, and other forms of clinical treatment are common. There is also a growing emphasis on holistic and integrative approaches, recognising the importance of lifestyle, environment, and community in mental health.

Eastern Perspectives

In many Eastern cultures, mental health is closely linked to spiritual and philosophical traditions. For example, in China and India, mental well-being is often associated with the balance of energies (Qi or Prana) and the harmony of mind, body, and spirit. Traditional practices such as meditation, yoga, acupuncture, and herbal medicine are widely used to promote mental health. Community and family support play a crucial role, and there is often a greater emphasis on collective well-being over individual well-being.

Indigenous Perspectives

Indigenous cultures around the world have unique understandings of mental health that are deeply connected to their cultural and spiritual beliefs. For instance, many Indigenous Australian communities view mental health through the lens of social and emotional well-being, which encompasses a holistic understanding of health that includes the spiritual, cultural, physical, and emotional dimensions of life. Healing practices often involve community rituals, connection to land, and traditional knowledge.

Global Challenges in Mental Health Care

Despite the cultural differences, many countries face similar challenges in addressing mental health issues. These challenges include stigma, lack of resources, and inadequate infrastructure.

Stigma and Discrimination

Stigma remains a significant barrier to mental health care globally. In many cultures, mental illness is still associated with shame, weakness, or moral failing, leading individuals to hide their conditions and avoid seeking help. Efforts to reduce stigma through education and awareness campaigns are critical in changing these attitudes.

Resource Allocation

Many countries, particularly low- and middle-income countries, struggle with limited resources for mental health care. This includes a shortage of trained mental health professionals, inadequate funding, and lack of facilities. International organisations, such as the World Health Organisation (WHO), are working to address these disparities by promoting global mental health initiatives and supporting capacity-building in these regions.

Infrastructure and Access to Care

Even in countries with more resources, access to mental health care can be a significant issue. Rural and remote areas often lack adequate services, and individuals may face long wait times or travel great distances to receive care. Telehealth and mobile health initiatives are emerging solutions to improve access, but these also require infrastructure and technological support.

Innovations and Approaches in Global Mental Health

Despite the challenges, there are many innovative approaches and successful initiatives in global mental health that provide valuable lessons and models for improvement.

Task-Shifting and Community Health Workers

In response to the shortage of mental health professionals, some countries have implemented task-shifting strategies, training community health workers to provide basic mental health care and support. For example, in Zimbabwe, the Friendship Bench project trains community health workers to offer problem-solving therapy to individuals with depression and anxiety. This approach has been successful in providing accessible care and reducing the burden on specialised services.

Integration of Mental Health into Primary Care

Integrating mental health services into primary care is another effective strategy. This approach ensures that mental health care is available at the first point of contact within the health system, making it more accessible and less stigmatised. Countries such as Chile and Uganda have successfully implemented integrated care models, improving early identification and treatment of mental health conditions.

Use of Technology

Technology offers promising solutions to many of the barriers in mental health care. Mobile apps, online counselling, and telepsychiatry can provide support and treatment to individuals in remote or underserved areas. In India, the Mental Health Care and Management System (MHCMS) uses a digital platform to track and manage patient data, improving care coordination and outcomes.

Culturally Adapted Interventions

Adapting mental health interventions to fit the cultural context is crucial for their success. This involves modifying therapeutic approaches to align with cultural beliefs and practices, as well as involving community members in the development and implementation of programs. For example, in Mexico, the MANAS project adapted cognitive-behavioural therapy to be delivered by lay health workers, with culturally relevant modifications to the content and delivery method.

International Organisations and Mental Health

Several international organisations are dedicated to improving global mental health through research, policy advocacy, and capacity-building initiatives.

World Health Organisation (WHO)

The WHO plays a leading role in global mental health, providing guidelines, conducting research, and supporting countries in developing and implementing mental health policies. The WHO's Mental Health Action Plan 2013-2020 aimed to promote mental well-being, prevent mental disorders, and provide comprehensive, integrated, and responsive mental health and social care services in community-based settings.

Mental Health Innovation Network (MHIN)

The MHIN is a global community of mental health innovators who share resources, ideas, and best practices. It supports the dissemination of evidence-based mental health interventions and encourages collaboration among researchers, practitioners, and policymakers.

Global Mental Health Action Network (GMHAN)

The GMHAN is a coalition of organisations and individuals working to improve global mental health. It focuses on advocacy, knowledge sharing, and capacity-building to address mental health challenges and promote effective, scalable solutions.

The Future of Global Mental Health

The future of global mental health lies in continued collaboration, innovation, and commitment to addressing the complex challenges that affect mental well-being. Key areas of focus include:

Reducing Stigma

Continued efforts to reduce stigma through education, media campaigns, and community engagement are essential for changing attitudes and encouraging help-seeking behaviour.

Expanding Access

Improving access to mental health care through innovative approaches such as task-shifting, telehealth, and integration into primary care will help to address gaps in service delivery and reach more individuals in need.

Enhancing Cultural Competence

Developing culturally competent mental health services that respect and incorporate local beliefs, practices, and values is crucial for the effectiveness and acceptance of interventions.

Strengthening Policy and Advocacy

Advocacy for stronger mental health policies, increased funding, and international support will help to build the infrastructure and resources needed for sustainable mental health care.

Promoting Research and Innovation

Investing in research to understand the diverse factors that influence mental health and developing innovative interventions will drive progress and improve outcomes.

Conclusion

Understanding global perspectives on mental health provides a rich tapestry of approaches, challenges, and innovations that can inform and inspire efforts to improve mental health care worldwide. By embracing cultural diversity, addressing common challenges, and learning from successful initiatives, we can work towards a future where mental health care is accessible, equitable, and effective for all. The journey towards better global mental health requires collaboration, commitment, and a shared vision of mental well-being as a fundamental human right.

CHAPTER 14: THE FUTURE OF MENTAL HEALTH ADVOCACY

Introduction

Mental health advocacy has made significant strides over the past few decades, contributing to increased awareness, reduced stigma, and improved access to mental health services. As we look to the future, it is essential to build on these successes and address the emerging challenges and opportunities in the field. This chapter explores the future of mental health advocacy, focusing on evolving strategies, technological advancements, policy developments, and the role of communities and individuals in fostering a more inclusive and supportive mental health landscape.

Evolving Strategies in Mental Health Advocacy

Integrating Mental Health into Mainstream Health Care

One of the primary goals for future mental health advocacy is to further integrate mental health into mainstream health care systems. This involves ensuring that mental health is given equal priority to physical health and that services are seamlessly incorporated into general health care settings.

Strategies:

- Promoting policies that mandate mental health screenings as part of routine health check-ups.

- Training general health care providers in basic mental health care and awareness.

- Developing integrated care models that provide comprehensive treatment plans addressing both mental and physical health needs.

Expanding Grassroots Movements

Grassroots movements have been instrumental in driving change and raising awareness at the community level. Future advocacy efforts should continue to empower local communities to take action and support mental health initiatives.

Strategies:

- Providing resources and training to community leaders and volunteers.

- Encouraging the establishment of local mental health support groups and networks.

- Supporting community-based mental health education and outreach programs.

Technological Advancements in Mental Health Advocacy

Digital Mental Health Platforms

The rapid advancement of technology presents new opportunities for mental health advocacy. Digital platforms can enhance access to information, support, and treatment for individuals worldwide.

Benefits:

- Increased accessibility for individuals in remote or underserved areas.

- Anonymity and privacy, reducing the stigma associated with seeking help.

- Flexibility in accessing support at any time.

Examples:

- Mobile apps offering mental health resources, self-help tools, and online counselling services.

- Virtual reality (VR) programs providing immersive therapeutic experiences.

- Artificial intelligence (AI) chatbots offering immediate support and crisis intervention.

Social Media and Awareness Campaigns

Social media has become a powerful tool for raising awareness and advocating for mental health. Future efforts can leverage these platforms to reach broader audiences and create more impactful campaigns.

Strategies:

- Using social media influencers to share personal stories and promote mental health awareness.

- Running targeted campaigns that address specific issues or populations.

- Creating interactive and engaging content, such as videos, infographics, and live discussions.

Policy Developments and Legislative Advocacy

Advocating for Comprehensive Mental Health Policies

Effective advocacy requires robust policies that protect and promote mental health. Future efforts should focus on advocating for comprehensive mental health legislation that addresses prevention, treatment, and support.

Key Policy Areas:

- Ensuring mental health parity, so mental health conditions receive the same level of care as physical health conditions.

- Expanding funding for mental health research, services, and workforce development.

- Implementing policies that support workplace mental health, including mental health leave and accommodations.

International Collaboration and Standards

Mental health advocacy can benefit from international collaboration and the establishment of global standards. Working together, countries can share best practices, resources, and innovations to improve mental health care worldwide.

Strategies:

- Supporting international agreements and frameworks that promote mental health.

- Participating in global mental health initiatives and networks.

- Advocating for the inclusion of mental health in international development goals and agendas.

The Role of Communities and Individuals

Building Resilient Communities

Communities play a crucial role in supporting mental health. Future advocacy should focus on building resilient communities that can provide support, reduce stigma, and promote mental well-being.

Strategies:

- Developing community-based mental health programs and resources.

- Encouraging community participation in mental health initiatives.

- Promoting social connections and supportive relationships within communities.

Empowering Individuals

Empowering individuals to take charge of their mental health is a vital component of future advocacy. This includes providing education, resources, and support to help people recognise and address mental health issues.

Strategies:

- Offering mental health education and literacy programs.

- Providing tools and resources for self-care and self-management of mental health.

- Encouraging individuals to become advocates and share their experiences to inspire others.

Embracing Diversity and Inclusivity

Addressing Disparities in Mental Health Care

Future mental health advocacy must address disparities in care and ensure that all individuals have access to the support they need. This involves recognising and addressing the unique needs of diverse populations.

Strategies:

- Promoting culturally competent mental health services.

- Advocating for policies that address social determinants of mental health, such as poverty, discrimination, and access to education.

- Supporting research that explores the mental health needs of underrepresented groups.

Promoting Inclusive Mental Health Practices

Inclusivity in mental health practices ensures that everyone, regardless of background or identity, feels supported and understood. Future advocacy should focus on creating inclusive environments that respect and value diversity.

Strategies:

- Developing mental health resources and services that are accessible and relevant to diverse populations.

- Training mental health professionals in cultural competency and inclusive practices.

- Encouraging inclusive language and behaviours in all aspects of mental health care and advocacy.

The Future of Mental Health Advocacy: A Vision

The future of mental health advocacy holds the promise of a world where mental health is universally recognised, respected, and supported. By embracing evolving strategies, leveraging technological advancements, advocating for comprehensive policies, and fostering inclusive and resilient communities, we can work towards this vision.

Key Goals:

- Achieving mental health parity with physical health in all health care systems.

- Ensuring universal access to high-quality mental health care and support.

- Eliminating stigma and discrimination associated with mental health conditions.

- Building a global movement that promotes mental well-being and empowers individuals to thrive.

Conclusion

The journey towards improved mental health advocacy is ongoing, requiring dedication, innovation, and collaboration. By focusing on the future and embracing new opportunities and challenges, we can continue to make progress in supporting mental health and well-being for all. The future of mental health advocacy is bright, and with concerted efforts, we can create a world where mental health is a priority, and everyone has the opportunity to live a fulfilling and healthy life.

CHAPTER 15: PERSONAL STORIES OF TRIUMPH AND RESILIENCE

Introduction

Personal stories have the power to inspire, educate, and ignite change. In the realm of mental health advocacy, personal narratives of triumph and resilience provide a profound testament to the human spirit's capacity to overcome challenges, navigate adversity, and thrive. This chapter showcases a collection of personal stories from individuals who have journeyed through mental health struggles, highlighting their experiences, insights gained, and the lessons they offer to others facing similar journeys.

Emma's Journey: Overcoming Depression Through Art Therapy

Emma's journey with depression began in her early twenties, marked by overwhelming feelings of sadness and hopelessness. Unable to find solace in conventional treatments, she discovered art therapy—a creative outlet that became her lifeline.

Emma's Reflection:

"Art therapy gave me a voice when words failed me. Through painting and sculpting, I could express emotions that seemed too heavy to bear. It wasn't about creating masterpieces but about connecting with myself on a deeper level."

Lesson Learned:

"Finding a creative outlet can be transformative. Whether it's painting, writing, or music, creativity can heal wounds that medicine alone cannot reach."

Raj's Story: From Stigma to Advocacy for Men's Mental Health

Raj's battle with anxiety began in his teens but intensified during his college years. Ashamed of seeking help, he suffered silently until a panic attack forced him to confront his condition. Now, he advocates for men's mental health, breaking down stereotypes and encouraging open dialogue.

Raj's Reflection:

"Speaking up was the hardest but most liberating thing I've ever done. It's not weak to ask for help—it's courageous. I want other men to know they're not alone and that seeking help is a sign of strength, not weakness."

Lesson Learned:

"Breaking stigma starts with conversation. By sharing our stories and vulnerabilities, we create a culture where mental health is seen as a priority, not a taboo."

Maria's Journey: Building Resilience After Trauma

Maria's journey with PTSD began after surviving a traumatic event. Through therapy, support groups, and a dedicated self-care routine, she has rebuilt her life and now supports others on their paths to healing.

Maria's Reflection:

"Recovery isn't linear. Some days are harder than others, but each step forward, no matter how small, is a victory. It's about learning to live with scars and finding strength in vulnerability."

Lesson Learned:

"Self-care isn't selfish—it's survival. Taking time to nurture your mind, body, and spirit is essential on the journey to healing."

David's Triumph: Overcoming Bipolar Disorder Through Peer Support

David's journey with bipolar disorder led him to discover the power of peer support. Connecting with others who understood his experiences provided validation, empathy, and hope on his path to stability.

David's Reflection:

"Peer support groups saved my life. They showed me that I wasn't alone and that recovery is possible. Sharing our struggles and successes reminds us that we're stronger together."

Lesson Learned:

"Finding a supportive community can make all the difference. Whether online or in person, knowing that others 'get it' can provide comfort and strength."

Conclusion: The Power of Personal Narratives

Each of these stories illustrates the resilience, courage, and hope that define the journey through mental health challenges. They remind us that recovery is possible, stigma can be overcome, and support is essential. By sharing these stories, we honour the voices of those who have bravely navigated darkness and emerged with wisdom to light the way for others.

Moving Forward Together

As we move forward in the realm of mental health advocacy, let us continue to amplify personal stories, celebrate triumphs, and support each other on the path to mental well-being. Together, we can build a future where everyone feels empowered to seek help, share their experiences, and live full, meaningful lives.